FOURTH EDITION

ADVANCED FETAL MONITORING COURSE

D0118190

Student Materials

AWHONN
Fetal Heart
Monitoring PROGRAM

AWHONN
PROMOTING THE HEALTH OF
WOMEN AND NEWBORNS

Kendall Hunt
publishing company

Cover image © JupiterImages Corporation, Inc.

www.kendallhunt.com
Send all inquiries to:
4050 Westmark Drive
Dubuque, IA 52004-1840

Printed in the United States of America
10 9 8 7 6 5

CONTENTS

INTRODUCTION AND SUPPLEMENTAL INFORMATION

Target Audience

The Advanced Fetal Heart Monitoring Course is based on educational theory. The instructional design incorporates critical thinking and decision making and is specifically designed for clinicians with previous fetal heart monitoring (FHM) experience. Residents, physicians, LPNs and LVNs may also participate in the course. Although prior completion of the Intermediate Fetal Heart Monitoring Course is not a requirement for Advanced Fetal Heart Monitoring Course attendance, AWHONN strongly recommends completion of a basic fetal monitoring course prior to attendance. To facilitate successful completion of the course, participants are expected, prior to attending the course, to review the current edition of the book *Fetal Heart Monitoring Principles and Practices*. Although the content of this course is comprehensive, specific patient care responsibilities vary according to institution, state, province or region. Participants of this course are advised to be familiar with their organizational/institutional responsibilities, as well as competence criteria and measurement.

Acknowledgment of Commercial Support

This CNE/CME activity has been created without commercial support.

Sponsorship and Co-Providership Statements

The CNE activity is provided by the Association of Women's Health, Obstetric and Neonatal Nurses (AWHONN) in collaboration with co-provider, Professional Education Services Group (PESG).

This activity has been planned and implemented in accordance with the essential areas and policies of the Accreditation Council for Continuing Medical Education (ACCME) through the joint sponsorship of the Professional Education Services Group (PESG) and the Association of Women's Health, Obstetric and Neonatal Nurses (AWHONN). The Professional Education Services Group is accredited by the ACCME to provide continuing medical education for physicians.

Learning Objectives

At the conclusion of this continuing education activity, participants will:

- Describe physiologic principles of maternal and fetal oxygen transfer and acid-base balance.
- Identify physiologic principles underlying fetal heart monitoring.
- Describe concepts in antenatal testing including analysis and interpretation of biophysical profiles and complex antenatal fetal heart monitoring tracings.
- Relate physiologic principles to the goals and interventions of antenatal testing.
- Evaluate interventions for patients undergoing antenatal testing.
- Analyze fetal cardiac arrhythmia patterns and describe outcomes associated with these patterns.
- Analyze complex fetal heart monitoring patterns utilizing current National Institute of Child Health and Development (NICHD)/American College of Obstetricians and Gynecologists (ACOG) FHM terminology and categories.
- Apply perinatal risk management principles, communication techniques and documentation strategies related to complex and challenging patient care scenarios.

Content Validation Statement

It is the policy of AWHONN and PESG to review and certify that the content contained in this CNE/CME activity is based on sound, scientific, evidence-based medicine. All recommendations involving clinical medicine in this CNE/CME activity are based on evidence that is accepted within the profession of medicine as adequate justification for their indications and contraindications in the care of patients. AWHONN and PESG further assert that all scientific research referred to, reported or used in this CNE/CME activity in support of or justification of a patient care recommendation conforms to the generally accepted standards of experimental design, data collection and analysis. Moreover, AWHONN and PESG establish that the content contained herein conforms to the definition of CNE as presented by the American Nurses Credentialing Center (ANCC) and the definition of CME as presented by the Accreditation Council for Continuing Medical Education (ACCME).

Disclosure Statement

It is the policy of AWHONN and PESG that the faculty and program planners and developers disclose real or apparent conflicts of interest relating to the topics of this education activity and also disclose discussion of unlabeled/unapproved uses of drugs or devices during their presentations. Detailed disclosures will be made available during the live program.

Conflict of Interest Resolution Statement

When individuals in a position to control content have reported financial, professional or personal relationships with one or more commercial interests, AWHONN and PESG will resolve such conflicts to ensure that the presentation is free from commercial bias. The content of this presentation was vetted by the following mechanisms and modified as required to meet this standard:

- Content peer review by external topic expert
- Content validation by external topic expert and internal AWHONN and PESG clinical staff

  Educational Peer Review Disclosure PESG reports the following:

- **George J. Vuturo, RPh, PhD**
  Vice President of Medical Affairs/CME Director
  Dr. Vuturo has no relevant financial relationships to disclose.
- **Lawrence Devoe, MD**
  Dr. Devoe has no relevant financial relationships to disclose.
- **Anne Santa-Donato, RNC, MSN**
  Director of Childbearing and Newborn Programs, AWHONN
  Ms. Santa-Donato has no relevant financial relationships to disclose.
- **Carol Elaine Brown, RN, BC, MN**
  Nurse Program Development Specialist, AWHONN
  Ms. Brown has no relevant financial relationships to disclose.

Accreditation Information

Association of Women's Health, Obstetric and Neonatal Nurses is accredited as a provider of continuing nursing education by the American Nurses Credentialing Center's Commission on Accreditation.

AWHONN also holds a California BRN number: California CNE provider #CEP580.

Accredited status does not imply endorsement by the provider or ANCC of any commercial products displayed or discussed in conjunction with an activity.

The maximum CNE credit that can be earned while attending the Advanced Fetal Heart Monitoring Course is eight (8) AWHONN contact hours. Participants must attend the entire course and complete the feedback document in order to receive the CNE credit.

Accreditation Statement—Physicians

Professional Education Services Group is accredited by the ACCME to provide continuing medical education for physicians.

Credit Designation Statement—Physicians

Professional Education Services Group designates this educational activity for a maximum of six (6) AMA PRA Category I Credits. Physicians should only claim credit within the extent of their participation in the activity.

DISCLAIMER

This course and all accompanying materials (publication) were developed by AWHONN, in cooperation with PESG, as an educational resource for fetal heart monitoring. It presents general methods and techniques of practice that are currently acceptable, based on current research and techniques used by recognized authorities. Proper care of individual patients may depend on many individual factors in clinical practice, as well as professional judgment in the techniques described herein. Clinical circumstances naturally vary, and professionals must use their own best judgment in accordance with the patients' needs and preferences, professional standards and institutional rules. Variations and innovations that are consistent with law, and that demonstrably improve the quality of patient care, should be encouraged.

AWHONN has sought to confirm the accuracy of the information presented herein and to describe generally accepted practices. However, AWHONN is not responsible for errors or omissions or for any consequences from application of the information in this resource and makes no warranty, expressed or implied, with respect to the contents of the publication.

Competent clinical practice depends on a broad array of personal characteristics, training, judgment, professional skills and institutional processes. This publication is simply one of many information resources. This publication is not intended to replace ongoing evaluation of knowledge and skills in the clinical setting. Nor has it been designed for use in hiring, promotion or termination decisions or in resolving legal disputes or issues of liability.

AWHONN believes that the drug selection and dosage set forth in this text are in accordance with current recommendations and practice at the time of publication. However, in view of ongoing research, changes in government regulations and the constant flow of information relating to drug therapy and drug reactions, the reader is urged to check other information available in other published sources for each drug to identify changes in indications, dosages, added warnings and precautions. This is particularly important when the recommended agent is a new or infrequently employed drug. In addition, appropriate medication use may depend on unique factors such as individuals' health status, other medication use and other factors which the professional must consider in clinical practice.

RESOURCES AND REFERENCE MATERIALS

The content of this section is intended to provide information about the NICHD definitions, descriptions of electronic fetal monitoring tracing characteristics and categories of the tracings.

Additional resources include documents that are published in the *Fetal Heart Monitoring Principles and Practices 4th edition* text:

- A table of parameters for scoring biophysical profile findings
- FHR Baseline Variability Definitions and Visual Interpretation Guide
- FHR Circles
- NICHD Descriptive Terms and Categories
- Decision Tree
- Three-Tier FHR Interpretation System

The Reference listing is intended to offer participants and Instructors additional resources for review in preparation for the Advanced Fetal Monitoring Course. Many participants have found these references valuable in developing guidelines and protocols for clinical practice. AWHONN FHM Instructors should review the references to support the course teaching materials and to prepare for potential questions by their course participants.

Also included is an answer sheet for Test B of the Advanced Fetal Monitoring Course. Test B is offered in the event the participant does not score the requisite 80% on Test A.

BASELINE VARIABILITY

The numbers (1) through (4) included in the following cells correspond to the numbers encircled on the Visual Assessment of Variability Scale.

Amplitude of FHR Change	Former AWHONN Baseline LTV Description	NICHD Baseline Variability Description
(1) Undetectable from baseline	Decreased/minimal	Absent
(2) Visually detectable from baseline, ≤5 bpm	Decreased/minimal	Minimal
(3) 6–25 bpm	Average/within normal limits	Moderate
(4) >25 bpm	Marked/saltatory	Marked

Adapted from Electronic fetal heart monitoring: Research guidelines for interpretation, National Institutes of Child Health and Human Development Research Planning Workshop, 1997, *Journal of Obstetric, Gynecologic and Neonatal Nursing, 26*(6), 635–640. Copyright: AWHONN.

Note: The exact language in the 1997 NICHD paper regarding minimal variability is "greater than undetectable" and less than or equal to 5 bpm. AWHONN has chosen the equivalent term "visually detectable" to clearly differentiate the definition of minimal variability from the definition of "absent variability," avoid confusion for users new to the NICHD terminology and emphasize the visual determination of variability.

The 2008 National Institute of Child Health and Human Development Workshop Report on Electronic Fetal Monitoring: Update on Definitions, Interpretation and Research Guidelines (2008) by Macones, G., Hankins, G., Spong, C., Haugh, J., and Moore, T., reconfirmed these definitions.

VISUAL ASSESSMENT OF VARIABILITY SCALE

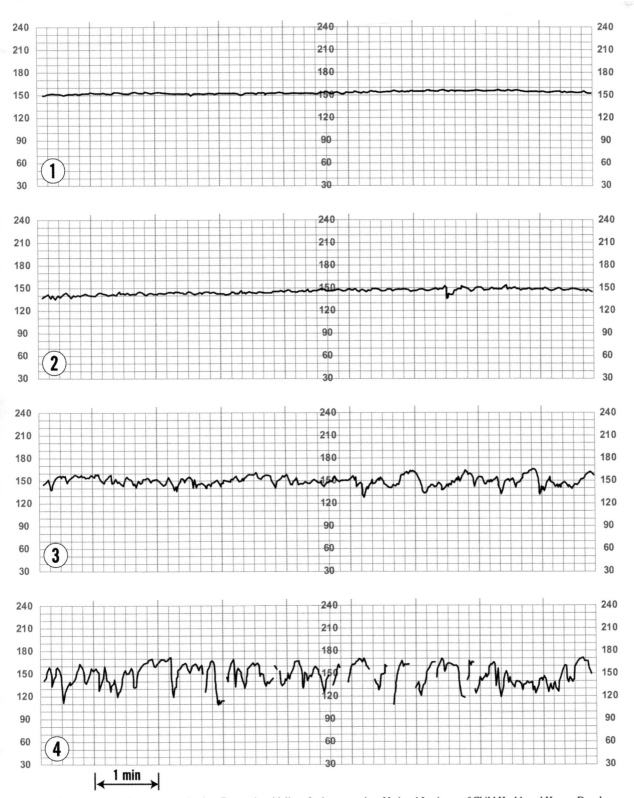

|← 1 min →|

Adapted from Electronic fetal heart monitoring: Research guidelines for interpretation, National Institutes of Child Health and Human Development Research Planning Workshop, 1997, *Journal of Obstetric, Gynecologic and Neonatal Nursing, 26*(6), 635–640. Copyright: AWHONN.

BIOPHYSICAL PROFILE INTERPRETATION AND SUGGESTED MANAGEMENT

Score	Interpretation	Management
8–10	Reassuring	• Consider increased frequency of testing or delivery if oligohydramnios is present
6	Equivocal	• Term fetus—consider delivery • Preterm fetus—retest within 12–24 hours • Consider increased frequency of testing or delivery if oligohydramnios is present
4 or less	Non-reassuring	• Further evaluation is indicated • Consider delivery

Adapted from American Academy of Pediatrics & The American College of Obstetricians and Gynecologists, 2007. Antepartum Care, Biophysical Profile. Elk Grove Village, IL: Authors.

FETAL HEART RATE CHARACTERISTICS AND PATTERNS: 2008 NICHD DESCRIPTIVE TERMS FOR FETAL HEART RATE CHARACTERISTICS

Term	Definition
Baseline Rate	Approximate mean FHR rounded to increments of 5 bpm during a 10-minute segment, excluding accelerations and decelerations and periods of marked variability. In any 10-minute window, the minimum baseline duration must be at least 2 minutes (not necessarily contiguous) or the baseline for that period is indeterminate. In this case, one may need to refer to the previous 10-minute segment for determination of the baseline.
Bradycardia	Baseline rate of <110 bpm.
Tachycardia	Baseline rate of >160 bpm.
Baseline Variability	Fluctuations in the baseline FHR are irregular in amplitude and frequency and are visually quantified as the amplitude of the peak to trough in bpm.
– Absent variability	Amplitude range undetectable.
– Minimal variability	Amplitude range visually detectable (>undetectable) but ≤5 bpm.
– Moderate variability	Amplitude range 6–25 bpm.
– Marked variability	Amplitude range >25 bpm.
Acceleration	Visually apparent ***abrupt*** increase (onset to peak is <30 seconds) in FHR above the adjacent baseline. The FHR peak is ≥15 bpm above the baseline and lasts ≥15 seconds but <2 minutes from the onset to return to baseline. Before 32 weeks of gestation, a peak ≥10 bpm above the baseline and duration of ≥10 seconds is an acceleration.
Prolonged Acceleration	Acceleration ≥2 minutes but <10 minutes duration.
Early Deceleration	Visually apparent, usually symmetrical ***gradual*** decrease (onset to nadir is ≥30 seconds) of the FHR and return to baseline associated with a uterine contraction. This decrease in FHR is calculated from the onset to the nadir of the deceleration. The nadir of deceleration occurs at the same time as the peak of the contraction. In most cases, the onset, nadir and recovery of the deceleration are coincident with the beginning, peak and ending of the contraction, respectively.

(continued)

Term	Definition
Late Deceleration	Visually apparent, usually symmetrical *gradual* decrease (onset to nadir is ≥30 seconds) of the FHR and return to baseline associated with a uterine contraction. This decrease is calculated from the onset to the nadir of the deceleration. It is delayed in timing, with the nadir of deceleration occurring after the peak of the contraction. In most cases, the onset, nadir and recovery of the deceleration occur after the onset, peak and ending of the contraction, respectively.
Variable Deceleration	Visually apparent *abrupt* decrease (onset to beginning of nadir is <30 seconds) in FHR below baseline. The decrease is calculated from the onset to the nadir of the deceleration. Decrease is ≥15 bpm, lasting ≥15 seconds but <2 minutes in duration. When variable decelerations are associated with uterine contractions, their onset, depth and duration vary with successive uterine contractions.
Prolonged Deceleration	Visually apparent decrease in FHR below baseline. Decrease is ≥15 bpm, lasting ≥2 minutes but <10 minutes from onset to return to baseline. A deceleration that lasts greater than or equal to 10 minutes is a baseline change.
Recurrent	Occurring with ≥50% of contractions in a 20-minute period.
Intermittent	Occurring with <50% of contractions in a 20-minute period.
Sinusoidal	Visually apparent undulating sine wave-like pattern in FHR baseline and cycle frequency of 3–5 per minute which persists for ≥20 minutes.

Macones, G. A., Hankins, G. D., Spong, C. Y., Hauth, J. D., & Moore, T. (2008). The 2008 National Institute of Child Health Human Development workshop report on electronic fetal monitoring: Update on definitions, interpretations, and research guidelines. *Obstetrics & Gynecology, 112*, 661–666; and *Journal of Obstetric, Gynecologic and Neonatal Nursing, 37*, 510–515.

2008 THREE-TIER FETAL HEART RATE INTERPRETATION SYSTEM

Category I

*Category I fetal heart rate (FHR) tracings include **all** of the following:*

- Baseline rate: 110–160 beats per minute (bpm)
- Baseline FHR variability: moderate
- Late or variable decelerations: absent
- Early decelerations: present or absent
- Accelerations: present or absent

Category II

Category II FHR tracings include all FHR tracings not categorized as Category I or Category III. Category II tracings may represent an appreciable fraction of those encountered in clinical care. Examples of Category II FHR tracings include any of the following:

Baseline Rate

- Bradycardia not accompanied by baseline variability
- Tachycardia

Baseline FHR Variability

- Minimal baseline variability
- Absent baseline variability not accompanied by recurrent decelerations
- Marked baseline variability

Accelerations
- Absence of induced accelerations after fetal stimulation

Periodic or Episodic Decelerations

- Recurrent variable decelerations accompanied by minimal or moderate baseline variability
- Prolonged deceleration ≥ 2 minutes but < 10 minutes
- Recurrent late decelerations with moderate baseline variability
- Variable decelerations with other characteristics, such as slow return to baseline, "overshoots," or "shoulders"

Category III

Category III FHR tracings include either

- Absent baseline FHR variability and any of the following:
  - Recurrent late decelerations
  - Recurrent variable decelerations
  - Bradycardia
- Sinusoidal pattern

Note: From: The 2008 National Institute of Child Health Human Development Workshop report on electronic fetal monitoring: Update on definitions, interpretations, and research guidelines, by G. A. Macones, G. D. Hankins, C. Y. Spong, J. D. Hauth, & T. Moore, 2008, *Journal of Obstetric, Gynecologic and Neonatal Nursing,* 37, 510–515; *Obstetrics & Gynecology,* 112, p. 665. Copyright 2008 by the American College of Obstetricians and Gynecologists. Reprinted with permission.

ALTERATIONS IN FHR CHARACTERISTICS
BY DYNAMIC PHYSIOLOGIC RESPONSE

Normal
Fetal Acid-Base Status: Well-Oxygenated Fetus

All of the following:
- Baseline rate: 110–160 bpm
- Baseline variability: moderate
- Late or variable decels: absent
- Early decels: present or absent
- Accels: present or absent

Category I

Indeterminate:
Compensatory Response

Examples:
- Moderate variability with recurrent late or variable decels
- Minimal variability with recurrent variable decels
- Absent variability without recurrent decels
- Bradycardia with moderate variability
- Prolonged decels
- Tachycardia

Category II

Abnormal Fetal
Acid-Base Status

Either:
- Absent variability with:
  --Recurrent late decels, or
  ---Recurrent variable decels, or
  ---Bradycardia

Or
- Sinusoidal pattern

Category III

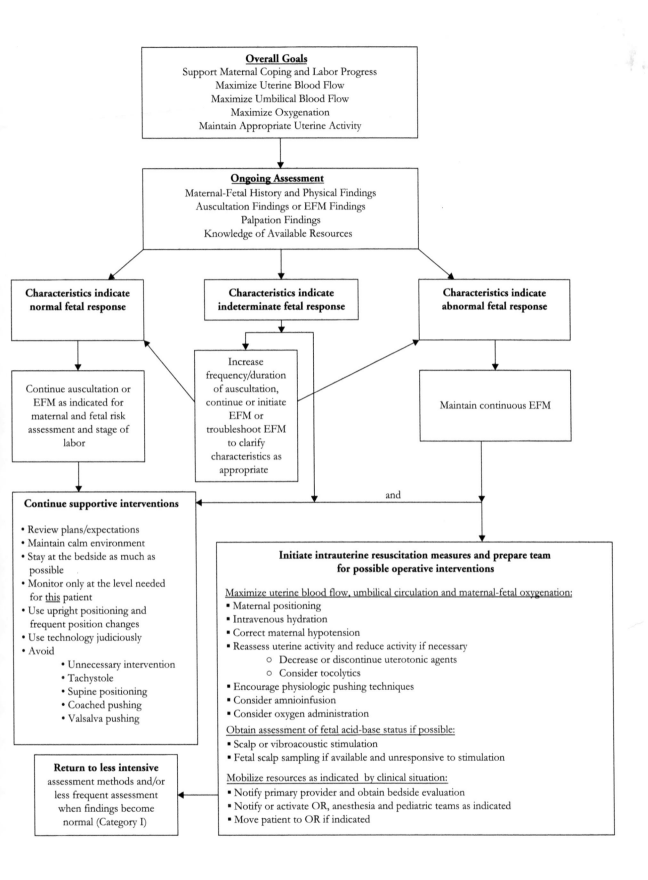

Overall Goals
Support Maternal Coping and Labor Progress
Maximize Uterine Blood Flow
Maximize Umbilical Blood Flow
Maximize Oxygenation
Maintain Appropriate Uterine Activity

Ongoing Assessment
Maternal-Fetal History and Physical Findings
Auscultation Findings or EFM Findings
Palpation Findings
Knowledge of Available Resources

Characteristics indicate normal fetal response

Characteristics indicate indeterminate fetal response

Characteristics indicate abnormal fetal response

Continue auscultation or EFM as indicated for maternal and fetal risk assessment and stage of labor

Increase frequency/duration of auscultation, continue or initiate EFM or troubleshoot EFM to clarify characteristics as appropriate

Maintain continuous EFM

and

Continue supportive interventions

• Review plans/expectations
• Maintain calm environment
• Stay at the bedside as much as possible
• Monitor only at the level needed for this patient
• Use upright positioning and frequent position changes
• Use technology judiciously
• Avoid
    • Unnecessary intervention
    • Tachystole
    • Supine positioning
    • Coached pushing
    • Valsalva pushing

Initiate intrauterine resuscitation measures and prepare team for possible operative interventions

Maximize uterine blood flow, umbilical circulation and maternal-fetal oxygenation:
▪ Maternal positioning
▪ Intravenous hydration
▪ Correct maternal hypotension
▪ Reassess uterine activity and reduce activity if necessary
    ○ Decrease or discontinue uterotonic agents
    ○ Consider tocolytics
▪ Encourage physiologic pushing techniques
▪ Consider amnioinfusion
▪ Consider oxygen administration

Obtain assessment of fetal acid-base status if possible:
▪ Scalp or vibroacoustic stimulation
▪ Fetal scalp sampling if available and unresponsive to stimulation

Mobilize resources as indicated by clinical situation:
▪ Notify primary provider and obtain bedside evaluation
▪ Notify or activate OR, anesthesia and pediatric teams as indicated
▪ Move patient to OR if indicated

Return to less intensive assessment methods and/or less frequent assessment when findings become normal (Category I)

REFERENCES

Fetal Oxygenation

American College of Obstetricians and Gynecologists. (2006). *Umbilical cord blood gas and acid-base analysis* (Committee Opinion No. 348). Washington, DC: Author.

American College of Obstetricians and Gynecologists. (2009). *Intrapartum fetal heart rate monitoring: Nomenclature, interpretation, and general management principles* (Practice Bulletin No. 106). Washington, DC: Author.

American College of Obstetricians and Gynecologists & American Academy of Pediatrics. (2003). *Neonatal encephalopathy and cerebral palsy: Defining the pathogenesis and pathophysiology.* Washington, DC: Author.

Bakker, P. C., Kurver, P. H., Kuik, D. J., & Van Geijn, H. P. (2007). Elevated uterine activity increases the risk of fetal acidosis at birth. *American Journal of Obstetrics and Gynecology, 196*, 313.e1–313.e6.

Blackburn, S. T. (2007). Prenatal period and placental physiology parturition and uterine physiology chapters. In *Maternal, Fetal & Neonatal Physiology: A Clinical Perspective.* St. Louis, MO: Saunders.

Brobowski, R. A. (2004). Maternal-fetal blood gas physiology. In G. A. Dildy, M. A. Belfort, G. R. Saade, J. P. Phelan, G. V. Hankins, & S. L. Clark (Eds.), *Critical care obstetrics,* (4th ed., pp. 43–59). Malde, MA: Blackwell Science.

Chambers, C., & Weiner, C. P. (2009). Teratogenesis and environmental exposure. In R. K. Creasy, R. Resnik, J. D. Iams, C. J. Lockwood, & T. R. Moore (Eds.), *Maternal-fetal medicine,* (6th ed., pp. 347–359). Philadelphia: Saunders.

Cleary-Goldman, J., Negron, M., Scott, J., Downing, R. A., Camann, W., Simpson, L., et al. (2005). Prophylactic ephedrine and combined spinal epidural. *Obstetrics and Gynecology, 106*, 466–472.

Fox, M., Kilpatrick, S., King, T., & Parer, J. T. (2000). Fetal heart rate monitoring: Interpretation and collaborative management. *Journal of Midwifery and Women's Health, 45*, 498–507.

Freeman, R. K., Garite, T. J., & Nageotte, M. P. (2003). *Fetal heart rate monitoring,* (3rd ed.). Philadelphia: Lippincott Williams & Wilkins.

Greiss, F. C., & Crandell, D. L. (1965). Therapy for hypotension induced by spinal anesthesia during pregnancy: Observations on gravid ewes. *Journal of American Medical Association, 191*, 793–796.

Harvey, C. J., & Chez, B. F. (1997). *Critical concepts in fetal monitoring,* (2nd ed.). Washington, DC: Association of Women's Health, Obstetric and Neonatal Nurses.

Hawkins, J. L., Goetzl, L., & Chesnut, D. H. (2007). Obstetric anesthesia. In S. G. Gabbe, J. R. Niebyl, & J. L. Simpson (Eds.), *Obstetrics: Normal and problem pregnancies,* (5th ed., pp. 396–427). Philadelphia: Churchill Livingstone.

Johnson, R. B. T, Gregory, K. D., & Niebyl, J. R. (2007). Preconception and prenatal care: Part of the continuum. In S. G. Gabbe, J. R. Niebyl, & J. L. Simpson (Eds.), *Obstetrics: Normal and problem pregnancies,* (5th ed., pp. 111–137). Philadelphia: Churchill Livingstone.

King, T., & Parer, J. (2000). The physiology of fetal heart rate patterns and perinatal asphyxia. *Journal of Perinatal and Neonatal Nursing, 14*, 19–39.

Kreiser, D., Katorza, E., Seidman, D. S., Etchin, A., & Schiff, E. (2004). The effect of ephedrine on intrapartum fetal heart rate after epidural analgesia. *Obstetrics and Gynecology, 104*, 1277–1281.

Kwee, A., Dekkers, A. H., van Wijk, H. P., van der Hoorn-van den Beld, C. W., & Visser, G. H (2007). Occurrence of ST-changes recorded with STAN® S21-monitor during normal and abnormal fetal heart rate patterns during labour. *European Journal of Obstetrics, Gynecology and Reproductive Biology, 135*, 28–34.

Lowe, N. K., & Reiss, R. (1996). Parturition and fetal adaptation. *Journal of Obstetric, Gynecologic and Neonatal Nursing, 25,* 339–349.

Macones, G. A., Hankins, G. D., Spong, C. Y., Hauth, J. D., & Moore, T. (2008). The 2008 National Institute of Child Health Human Development workshop report on electronic fetal monitoring: Update on definitions, interpretation, and research guidelines. *Obstetrics & Gynecology, 112,* 661–666; and *Journal of Obstetric, Gynecologic and Neonatal Nursing, 37,* 510–515.

March of Dimes. (2009). Cerebral palsy. Available at http://www.marchofdimes.com/pnhec/4439_1208.asp. Retrieved May 27, 2009.

McCance, K. L., & Huether, S. E. (2006). *Pathophysiology: The biologic basis for disease in adults and children,* (5th ed.). St. Louis: Mosby.

Meschia, G. (1979). Supply of oxygen to the fetus. *Journal of Reproductive Medicine, 23,* 160–165.

Meschia, G. (2009). Placental respiratory gas exchange and fetal oxygenation. In R. K. Creasy, R. Resnik, J. D. Iams, C. J. Lockwood, & T. R. Moore (Eds.), *Maternal-fetal medicine* (6th ed., pp. 181–191). Philadelphia: Saunders.

Nageotte, M. P., & Gilstrap, L. C. (2009). Intrapartum fetal surveillance. In R. K. Creasy, R. Resnik, J. D. Iams, C. J. Lockwood, & T. R. Moore (Eds.), *Maternal-fetal medicine,* (6th ed., pp. 398–417). Philadelphia: Saunders.

National Institute of Neurological Disorders and Stroke. (2009). NINDS Cerebral Palsy Information Page. Available from http://www.ninds.nih.gov/disorders/cerebral_palsy/cerebral_palsy.htm Retrieved May 27, 2007

Neoventa. (2008). *Fetal monitoring and ST analysis.* Chicago: Author.

Niebyl, J. R., & Simpson, J. L. (2007). Drugs and environmental agents in pregnancy and lactation: Embryology, teratology, epidemiology. In S. G. Gabbe, J. R. Niebyl, & J. L. Simpson (Eds.), *Obstetrics: Normal and problem pregnancies,* (5th ed., pp. 184–214). Philadelphia: Churchill Livingstone.

Parer, J. T. (1997). *Handbook of fetal heart rate monitoring* (2nd ed.). Philadelphia: Saunders.

Parer, J. T., King, T., Flanders, S., Fox, M., & Kilpatrick, S. J. (2006). Fetal acidemia and electronic fetal heart rate patterns: Is there evidence of an association. *Journal of Maternal-Fetal and Neonatal Medicine, 19,* 289–294.

Price, S. A., & Wilson, L. M. (2003). *Pathophysiology: Clinical concepts of disease processes* (6th ed.). St. Louis: Mosby.

Rosen, K. G. (2005). Fetal electrocardiogram waveform analysis in labour. *Current Opinion in Obstetrics and Gynecology, 17,* 147–150.

Rosen, K. G., Amer-Whalen, I., Luzietti, R., & Noren, H. (2004). Fetal ECG waveform analysis. *Best Practice & Research Clinical Obstetrics & Gynaecology, 18,* 485–514.

Simpson, K. R., & James, D. (2005). Efficacy of intrauterine resuscitation techniques in improving fetal oxygen status in labor. *Obstetrics and Gynecology, 105,* 1362–1368

Simpson, K. R., & James, D. C. (2008). Effects of oxytocin-induced uterine hyperstimulation on fetal oxygen status and fetal heart rate patterns during labor. *American Journal of Obstetrics and Gynecology, 199,* 34.e1–34.e5.

Society of Obstetricians and Gynaecologists of Canada. (2007). Fetal health surveillance: Antepartum and intrapartum consensus guidelines in (SOGC Clinical Practice Guidelines No. 197). *Journal of Obstetrics and Gynaecology in Canada, 29*(9), S3–S56.

Tucker, S. M., Miller, L. A., & Miller, D. A. (2009). *Fetal monitoring: A multidisciplinary approach,* (6th ed.). St. Louis: Mosby.

Antepartum Fetal Testing

American College of Obstetricians and Gynecologists Committee on Practice Bulletins—Obstetrics. (1999). Reaffirmed 2009. Antepartum fetal surveillance. (ACOG Practice Bulletin No. 9). Washington, DC: Author.

Anyaegbunam, A., Brustman, L., Divon, M., & Langer, O. (1986). The significance of antepartum variable decelerations. *American Journal of Obstetrics and Gynecology, 155,* 707–710.

Armour, K. (2004). Antepartum maternal-fetal assessment. *AWHONN Lifelines, 8,* 232–240.

Association of Women's Health, Obstetric, and Neonatal Nurses. (2009). *Ultrasound examinations performed by nurses in OB, GYN & reproductive medicine settings: Clinical competencies and education guide,* (3rd ed.). Washington, DC: Author.

Babazadeh, R., Abdali, K., Lotfalizadeh, M., Tabatabaie, H., & Kaviani, M. (2005). Diurnal nonstress test variations in the human fetus at risk. *International Journal of Gynecology and Obstetrics, 90,* 189–192.

Bashat, A. A. (2006). Fetal growth disorders. In D. K. James, P. J. Steer, C. P. Weiner, & B. Gonik (Eds.), *High risk pregnancy management options,* (3rd ed., pp. 240–271). Philadelphia: Saunders.

Benirschke, K., Kaufman, P., & Baergen, N. (2006). Anatomy and pathology of the umbilical cord. In K. Benirschke, P. Kaufman, & N. Baeren (Eds.), *Pathology of the human placenta,* (5th ed., pp. 380–451). New York: Springer.

Bishop, E. H. (1981). Fetal acceleration test. *American Journal of Obstetrics and Gynecology, 141,* 905–909.

Bobby, P. (2003). Multiple assessment techniques evaluate antepartum fetal risks. *Pediatric Annals, 32,* 609–617.

Brown, R., & Patrick, J. (1981). The nonstress test: How long is enough? *American Journal of Obstetrics and Gynecology, 141,* 646–651.

Clark, S. L., Gimovsky, M. L., & Miller, F. C. (1982). Fetal heart rate response to scalp blood sampling. *American Journal of Obstetrics and Gynecology, 144,* 706–708.

Clark, S. L., Gimovsky, M. L., & Miller, F. C. (1984). The scalp stimulation test: A clinical alternative to fetal scalp blood sampling. *American Journal of Obstetrics and Gynecology, 148,* 274–277.

Deren, O., Karaer, C., Onderoglu, L., Yigit, N., Durukan, T., & Bahado-Singh, R. (2001). The effect of steroids on the biophysical profile and Doppler indices of umbilical and middle cerebral arteries in healthy preterm fetuses. *European Journal of Obstetrics and Gynecology and Reproductive Biology, 99,* 72–76.

Devoe, L. D. (1982). Antepartum fetal heart rate testing in preterm pregnancy. *Obstetrics and Gynecology, 60,* 431–436.

Devoe, L. D. (2008). Antenatal fetal assessment: Contraction stress test, nonstress test, vibroacoustic stimulation, amniotic fluid volume, biophysical profile, and modified biophysical profile: An overview. *Seminars in Perinatology, 32,* 247–252.

Druzin, M. L., Fox, A., Kogut, E., & Carlson, C. (1985). The relationship of the nonstress test to gestational age. *American Journal of Obstetrics and Gynecology, 153,* 386–389.

Druzin, M. L., Smith, J. F., Gabbe, S. G., & Reed, K. L. (2007). Antepartum fetal evaluation. In S. G. Gabbe, J. R. Niebyl, & J. L. Simpson (Eds.), *Obstetrics: Normal and problem pregnancies,* (5th ed., pp. 267–300). Philadelphia: Churchill Livingstone.

Elimian, A., Figueroa, R., & Tejani, N. (1997). Intrapartum assessment of fetal well-being: A comparison of scalp stimulation with scalp blood pH sampling. *Obstetrics and Gynecology, 89,* 373–376.

Freeman, R. K. (1975). The use of the oxytocin challenge test for antepartum clinical evaluation of uteroplacental respiratory function. *American Journal of Obstetrics and Gynecology, 121,* 481–489.

Freeman, R. K., Anderson, G., & Dorchester, W. (1982). A prospective multi-institutional study of antepartum fetal heart rate monitoring: Risk of perinatal mortality and morbidity according to antepartum fetal heart rate test results. *American Journal of Obstetrics and Gynecology, 143,* 771–777.

Freeman, R. K., Garite, T. J., & Nageotte, M. P. (2003). *Fetal heart rate monitoring* (3rd ed.). Philadelphia: Lippincott Williams & Wilkins.

Froen, J. F. (2004). A kick from within: Fetal movement counting and the cancelled progress in antenatal care. *Journal of Perinatal Medicine, 32*, 13–24.

Froen, J. F., Heazell, A. E. P., Tveit, J. V. H., Saasted, E., Fretts, R. C., & Flenady, V. (2008). Fetal movement assessment. *Seminars in Perinatology, 32*, 243–246.

Gegor, C. L., Paine, L. L., Costigan, K., & Johnson, T. R. B. (1994). Interpretation of biophysical profiles by nurses and physicians. *Journal of Obstetric, Gynecologic, and Neonatal Nursing, 23*, 405–410.

Ghidini, A., & Locatelli, A. (2008). Monitoring fetal well-being: Role of uterine artery doppler. *Seminars in Perinatology, 32*, 258–262.

Goodman, J. D. S., Visser, F. G. A., & Dawes, G. S. (2005). Effects of maternal cigarette smoking on fetal trunk movements, fetal breathing movements, and the fetal heart rate. *British Journal of Obstetrics and Gynaecology, 91*, 657–661.

Harman, C. R. (2009). Assessment of fetal health. In R. K. Creasy, R. Resnik, J. D. Iams, C. J. Lockwood, & T. R. Moore (Eds.), *Maternal-fetal medicine,* (6th ed., pp. 361–395). Philadelphia: Saunders.

Kelly, M. K., Schneider, E. P., Petrikovsky, B. M., & Lesser, M. L. (2000). Effect of antenatal steroid administration on the fetal biophysical profile. *Journal of Clinical Ultrasound, 28*, 224–226.

King, T., & Parer, J. (2000). The physiology of fetal heart rate patterns and perinatal asphyxia. *Journal of Perinatal and Neonatal Nursing, 14*, 19–39.

Kontopoulos, E. V., & Vintzileos, A. (2004). Condition specific antepartum fetal testing. *American Journal of Obstetrics and Gynecology, 191*, 1546–1551.

Lavin, J. P., Miodovnik, M., & Barden, T. P. (1984). Relationship of nonstress test reactivity and gestational age. *Obstetrics and Gynecology, 63*, 338–344.

Lenke, R. R., & Nemes, J. M. (1984). Use of nipple stimulation to obtain contraction stress test. *Obstetrics and Gynecology, 63*, 345–348.

Lyndon, A. & Ali, L. (2009). *Fetal heart monitoring: Principles and practices* (4th ed.). Dubuque, IA: Kendall Hunt.

Macones, G. A., Hankins, G. D., Spong, C. Y., Hauth, J. D., & Moore, T. (2008). The 2008 National Institute of Child Health Human Development workshop report on electronic fetal monitoring: Update on definitions, interpretations, and research guidelines. *Obstetrics & Gynecology, 112*, 661–666; and *Journal of Obstetric, Gynecologic and Neonatal Nursing, 37*, 510–515.

Manning, F. A., Baskett, T. F., Morrison, I., & Lange, I. (1981). Fetal biophysical scoring: A prospective study in 1,184 high risk patients. *American Journal of Obstetrics and Gynecology, 140*, 289–294.

McCarthy, K. E., & Narrigan, D. (1995). Is there scientific support for the use of juice to facilitate the nonstress test? *Journal of Obstetric, Gynecologic, and Neonatal Nursing, 24*, 303–307.

Meis, P. J., Ureda, J. R., Swain, M., Kelly, R. T., Penry, M., & Sharp, P. (1986). Variable decelerations during nonstress tests are not a sign of fetal compromise. *American Journal of Obstetrics and Gynecology, 154*, 586–590.

Menihan, C. A. (2000). Limited obstetric ultrasound in nursing practice. *Journal of Obstetric, Gynecologic, and Neonatal Nursing, 29*, 325–330.

Miller, D. A., Rabello, Y. A., & Paul, R. H. (1996). The modified biophysical profile: Antepartum testing in the 1990s. *American Journal of Obstetrics and Gynecology, 174*, 812–817.

Miller, F. C., Skiba, H., & Klapholz, H. (1978). The effect of maternal blood sugar levels on fetal activity. *Obstetrics and Gynecology, 52*, 662–665.

Mirghani, H. M., Weerasinghe, D. S., Ezimokhai, M., & Smith, J. R. (2003). The effect of maternal fasting on the fetal biophysical profile. *International Journal of Gynecology and Obstetrics, 81*, 17–21.

Niebyl, J. R., & Simpson, J. L. (2007). Drugs and environmental agents in pregnancy and lactation: Embryology, teratology, epidemiology. In S. G. Gabbe, J. R. Niebyl, & J. L. Simpson (Eds.), *Obstetrics: Normal and problem pregnancies,* (5th ed., pp. 184–214). Philadelphia: Churchill Livingstone.

O' Leary, J. A., Andrinopoulos, G. C., & Giordano, P. C. (1980). Variable decelerations and the nonstress test: An indication of cord compromise. *American Journal of Obstetrics and Gynecology, 137,* 704–706.

Oncken, C., Kranzler, H., O'Malley, P., Gendreau, P., & Campbell, W. A. (2002). The effect of cigarette smoking on fetal heart rate characteristics. *Obstetrics and Gynecology, 99,* 751–755.

Papoutsis, J., & Kroumpouzos, G. (2007). Dermatologic disorders of pregnancy. In S. G. Gabbe, J. R. Niebyl, & J. L. Simpson (Eds.), *Obstetrics: Normal and problem pregnancies*, (5th ed., pp. 1178–1192). Philadelphia: Churchill Livingstone.

Patrick, J., Campbell, K., Carmichael, L., Natale, R., & Richardson, B. (1982). Patterns of gross fetal body movements over 24-hour observation intervals during the last 10 weeks of pregnancy. *American Journal of Obstetrics and Gynecology, 142,* 363–371.

Phelan, J. P., Kester, R., & Labudovich, M. L. (1982). Nonstress test and maternal serum glucose determinations. *Obstetrics and Gynecology, 60,* 437–439.

Phelan, J. P., & Lewis, P. E. (1981). Fetal heart rate decelerations during a nonstress test. *Obstetrics and Gynecology, 57,* 228–232.

Pietrantoni, M., Angel, J. L., Parsons, M. T., McClain, L., Arango, H. A., & Spellacy, W. N. (1991). Human fetal response to vibroacoustic stimulation as a function of stimulus duration. *Obstetrics and Gynecology, 78,* 807–811.

Ray, M., Freeman, R., Pine, S., & Hesselgesser, R. (1972). Clinical experience with the oxytocin challenge test. *American Journal of Obstetrics and Gynecology, 114,* 1–9.

Reece, E. A., Hagay, Z., Roberts, A. B., DeGennaro, N., Homko, C. J., Connolly-Diamond, M., et al. (1995). Fetal doppler and behavioural responses during hypoglycemia induced with the insulin clamp technique in pregnant diabetic women. *American Journal of Obstetrics and Gynecology, 172,* 151–155.

Reed, K. L. (1997). Doppler: The fetal circulation. *Clinical Obstetrics and Gynecology, 40,* 750–754.

Roberts, A. B., Little, D., Cooper, D., & Campbell, S. (1979). Normal patterns of fetal activity in the third trimester. *British Journal of Obstetrics and Gynaecology, 86,* 4–9.

Rotmensch, S., Liberati, M., Vishne, T. H., Celentano, C., Ben-Rafael, Z. & Bellati, U. (1999). The effects of betamethasone and dexamethasone on fetal heart rate patterns and biophysical activities: A prospective randomized trial. *Acta Obstetricia et Gynecologica Scandinavia, 78,* 493–500.

Sarno, A. P., & Bruner, J. P. (1990). Fetal acoustic stimulation as a possible adjunct to diagnostic obstetric ultrasound: A preliminary report. *Obstetrics and Gynecology, 76,* 668–670.

Senat, M. V., Minoui, S., Multon, O., Fernandez, H., Frydman, R., & Ville, Y. (1998). Effect of dexamethasone and betamethasone on fetal heart rate variability in preterm labour: A randomized study. *British Journal of Obstetrics and Gynecology, 105,* 749–755.

Signore, C., Freeman, R. K., & Spong, C. Y. (2009). Antenatal testing: A reevaluation. *Obstetrics & Gynecology, 113,* 687–701.

Smith, C. V., Phelan, J. P., Paul, R. H., & Broussard, P. (1985). Fetal acoustic stimulation testing: A retrospective experience with the fetal acoustic stimulation test. *American Journal of Obstetrics and Gynecology, 153,* 567–569.

Smith, C. V., Phelan, J. P., Platt, L. D., Broussard, P., & Paul, R. H. (1986). Fetal acoustic stimulation testing II: A randomized clinical comparison with the nonstress test. *American Journal of Obstetrics and Gynecology, 155*, 131–134.

Society of Obstetricians and Gynaecologists of Canada. (2007). Fetal health surveillance: Antepartum and intrapartum consensus guidelines in (SOGC Clinical Practice Guidelines No. 197). *Journal of Obstetrics and Gynaecology in Canada, 29*, S3–S56.

Stringer, M., Miesnik, S. R., Brown, L. P., Menei, L., & Macones, G. A. (2003). Limited obstetric ultrasound examinations: Competency and cost. *Journal of Obstetric, Gynecologic, and Neonatal Nursing, 32*, 307–312.

Thaler, I., Goodman, J. D., & Dawes, G. S. (1980). Effects of maternal cigarette smoking on fetal breathing and fetal movements. *American Journal of Obstetrics and Gynecology, 138*, 282–287.

Vintzileos, A. M., Campbell, W. A., Ingardia, C. J., & Nochimson, D. (1983). The biophysical profile and its predictive value. *Obstetrics and Gynecology, 62*, 271–278.

Vintzileos, A. M., Fleming, A. D., Scorza, W. E., Wolf, E. J., Balducci, J., Campbell, W. A., & Rodis, J. F. (1991). Relationship between fetal biophysical activities and cord blood gas values. *American Journal of Obstetrics and Gynecology, 165*, 707–713.

Vintzileos, A. M., Gaffney, S. E., Salinger, L. M., Kontopoulos, V. G., Campbell, W. A., & Nochimson, D. J. (1987). The relationships among the fetal biophysical profile, umbilical cord pH, and Apgar scores. *American Journal of Obstetrics and Gynecology, 157*, 627–631.

Fetal Arrythmias

Blackburn, S. (2007). *Maternal, fetal, and neonatal physiology: A clinical perspective,* (3rd ed., pp. 287–296). St. Louis: Saunders.

Centers for Disease Control and Prevention. (2002). *Prevention of perinatal group B streptococcal disease. MMWR: Recommendations and Reports, 51, RR11*. Available at www.cdc.gov/mmwr/preview/mmwrhtml/rr5111a1.htm Retrieved March 19, 2009.

Copel, J. A., Liang, R. I., Demasio, K., Ozeren, S., & Kleinman, C. S. (2000). The clinical significance of the irregular fetal heart rhythm. *American Journal of Obstetrics and Gynecology, 182*, 813–819.

Fineman, J. R., & Clyman, R. (2009). Fetal cardiovascular physiology. In R. K. Creasy, R. Resnik, J. D. Iams, C. J. Lockwood, & T. R. Moore (Eds.), *Maternal-fetal medicine,* (6th ed., pp. 159–170).

France, R. (2006). A review of fetal circulation and the segmental approach in fetal echocardiography. *Journal of Diagnostic Medical Sonography, 22*, 29–39.

Freeman, R. K., Garite, T. J., & Nageotte, M. P. (2003). *Fetal heart monitoring,* (3rd ed.). Philadelphia: Lippincott, Williams, & Wilkins.

Garite, T. J. (2007). Intrapartum fetal evaluation. In S. G. Gabbe, J. R. Niebyl, & J. L. Simpson (Eds.), *Obstetrics: Normal and problem pregnancies,* (5th ed., pp. 364–395). Philadelphia: Churchill Livingstone.

Hameed, A. B., & Sklansky, M. S. (2007). Pregnancy: Maternal and fetal heart disease. *Current Problems in Cardiology, 32*, 419–494.

Handley, M., & Collins, A. (2008). Delicate threads: Autoimmune complications in a high risk pregnancy. *Nursing for Women's Health, 12*, 139–145.

Jaeggi, E., Fouron, J., & Drblik, S. (1998). Fetal atrial flutter: Diagnosis, clinical features, treatment, and outcome. *The Journal of Pediatrics, 132*, 335–339.

Jaeggi, E. T., & Nii, M. (2005). Fetal brady- and tachyarrhythmias: New and accepted diagnostic and treatment methods. *Seminars in Fetal and Neonatal Medicine, 10*, 504–514.

Kiserud, T. (2005). Physiology of the fetal circulation. *Seminars in Fetal and Neonatal Medicine, 10*, 493–503.

Kleinman, C. S. (2006). Prenatal cardiac therapy. In M. I. Evans, M. P. Johnson, Y. Yaron, & A. Drugan (Eds.), *Prenatal diagnosis* (pp. 671–682). New York: McGraw-Hill.

Kleinman, C. S., & Nehgme, R. A. (2004). Cardiac arrhythmias in the human fetus. *Pediatric Cardiology, 25,* 234–251.

Larmay, H. J., & Strasburger, J. F. (2004). Differential diagnosis and management of the fetus and newborn with an irregular or abnormal heart rate. *Pediatric Clinics of North America, 51,* 1033–1050.

Lockshin, M. D., Salmon, J. E., & Erkan, D. (2009). Pregnancy and rheumatic diseases. In R. K. Creasy, R. Resnik, J. D. Iams, C. J. Lockwood, & T. R. Moore (Eds.), *Maternal-fetal medicine,* (6th ed., (pp.1080–1087). Philadelphia: Saunders.

Macones, G. A., Hankins, G. D., Spong, C. Y., Hauth, J. D., & Moore, T. (2008). The 2008 National Institute of Child Health Human Development workshop report on electronic fetal monitoring: Update on definitions, interpretations, and research guidelines. *Obstetrics & Gynecology, 112,* 661–666; and *Journal of Obstetric, Gynecologic and Neonatal Nursing, 37,* 510–515.

Mecacci, F., Pieralli, A., Bianchi, B., & Paidas, M. J. (2007). The impact of autoimmune disorders and adverse pregnancy outcome. *Seminars in Perinatology, 31,* 223–226.

Mielke, G., & Benda, N. (2001). Cardiac output and central distribution of blood flow in the human fetus. *Circulation, 103,* 1662–1668.

Nageotte, M. P., & Gilstrap, L. C. (2009). Intrapartum fetal surveillance. In R. K. Creasy, R. Resnik, J. D. Iams, C. J. Lockwood, & T. R. Moore (Eds.), *Maternal-Fetal Medicine,* (6th ed., pp. 398–417). Philadelphia: Saunders.

Oudijk, M. A., Michon, M. M., Kleinman, C. S., Kapusta, L., Stoutenbeek, P., Visser, G. H., et al. (2000). Sotalol to treat fetal dysrhythmias. *Circulation, 101,* 2721–2726.

Parker, L. A. (2006). Hydrops fetalis. *Newborn and Infant Nursing Reviews, 6,* e1–e8.

Pedra, S. R., Smallhorn, J. F., Ryan, G., Chitayat, D., Taylor, G. P., Khan, R., et al. (2002). Fetal cardiomyopathies: Pathogenic mechanisms, hemodynamic findings, and clinical outcome. *Circulation, 106,* 585–591.

Rychik, J. (2006a). Evaluation of the fetal cardiovascular system. In M. I. Evans, M. P. Johnson, Y. Yaron, & A. Drugan (Eds.), *Prenatal diagnosis* (pp. 653–699). New York: McGraw-Hill.

Rychik, J. (2006b). Fetal cardiovascular physiology. *Pediatric Cardiology, 25,* 201–209.

Simpson, J. M. (2006). Fetal arrhythmias. *Ultrasound in Obstetrics and Gynecology, 27,* 599–606.

Simpson, J. M., & Sharland, G. K. (1998). Fetal tachycardias: Management and outcome of 127 consecutive cases. *Heart, 79,* 576–578.

Simpson, K. R. (2008). Intrauterine resuscitation during labor: Should maternal oxygen administration be a first-line measure? *Seminars in Fetal and Neonatal Medicine, 13,* 362–367.

Simpson, K. R. (2009). Physiologic interventions for fetal heart rate patterns. In A. Lyndon & L. Usher Ali (Eds.) *Fetal heart monitoring: Principles and practices,* (4th ed.). Dubuque, IA: Kendall Hunt.

Singh, G. K. (2004). Management of fetal tachycardia. Current Treatment Options in *Cardiovascular Medicine, 6,* 399–406.

Sklansky, M. (2009). Fetal cardiac malformations and arrhythmias: Detection, diagnosis, management, and prognosis. In R. K. Creasy, R. Resnik, J. D. Iams, C. J. Lockwood, & T. R. Moore (Eds.), *Maternal-fetal medicine,* (6th ed., pp. 306–345). Philadelphia: Saunders.

Smeltzer, S. C., Bare, B. G., Hinkle, J. L. & Cheever, K. H., (2008). *Brunner and Suddarth's textbook of medical-surgical nursing,* (11th ed., pp. 1856–1869). New York: Lippincott, Williams, and Wilkins.

Society of Obstetricians and Gynaecologists of Canada. (2002). Fetal health surveillance: Antepartum and intrapartum consensus guidelines in (SOGC Clinical Practice

Guidelines No. 197). *Journal of Obstetrics and Gynaecology in Canada, 29,* S3–S56.

Strasburger, J. F., Cheulkar, B., & Wichman, H. J. (2007). Perinatal arrhythmias: Diagnosis and management. *Clinics in Perinatology, 34,* 627–652.

Trines, J., & Hornberger, L. K. (2004). Evolution of heart disease in utero. *Pediatric Cardiology, 25,* 287–298.

Tucker, S. M., Miller, L. A., & Miller, D. A. (2009). *Fetal monitoring: A multidisciplinary approach,* (6th ed.). St. Louis: Mosby.

Wren, C. (2006). Cardiac arrhythmias in the fetus and newborn. Seminars in Fetal and *Neonatal Medicine, 11,* 182–190.

Complex Case Studies

American Academy of Pediatrics & American College of Obstetricians and Gynecologists. (2007). *Guidelines for perinatal care* (6th ed.). Elk Grove Village, IL: Authors.

American College of Obstetricians and Gynecologists (ACOG). (2002). *Diagnosis and management of preeclampsia and eclampsia* (Practice Bulletin No. 33). Washington, DC: Author.

American College of Obstetricians and Gynecologists (ACOG). (2003a). *Cervical insufficiency* (Practice Bulletin No. 48). Washington, DC: Author.

American College of Obstetricians and Gynecologists (ACOG). (2003b). *Nonobstetric surgery in pregnancy* (Committee Opinion No. 284). Washington, DC: Author.

American College of Obstetricians and Gynecologists (ACOG). (2004). *Vaginal birth after previous cesarean delivery* (Practice Bulletin No. 54). Washington, DC: Author.

American College of Obstetricians and Gynecologists (ACOG). (2006). *Induction of labor for vaginal birth after cesarean delivery* (Committee Opinion 342). Washington, DC: Author.

American College of Obstetricians and Gynecologists (ACOG). (2009a). *Critical care in pregnancy* (Practice Bulletin No. 100). Washington, DC: Author.

American College of Obstetricians and Gynecologists. (2009b). *Induction of labor* (Practice Bulletin No. 107). Washington, DC: Author.

American College of Obstetricians and Gynecologists. (2009c). *Intrapartum fetal heart rate monitoring: Nomenclature, interpretation, and general management principles* (Practice Bulletin No. 106). Washington, DC: Author.

American College of Obstetricians and Gynecologists (ACOG). (2009d). *Prevention of early onset Group B Streptococcal disease in newborns* (Committee Opinion No. 270). Washington, DC: Author.

American College of Obstetricians and Gynecologists & American Academy of Pediatrics. (2003). *Neonatal encephalopathy and cerebral palsy: Defining the pathogenesis and pathophysiology.* Washington, DC: Author.

Ayres, A. W., Johnson, T. R. B., & Hayashi, R. (2001). Characteristics of fetal heart rate tracings prior to uterine rupture. *International Journal of Gynaecology and Obstetrics, 74,* 235–240.

Baird, S. M., & Ruth, D. J. (2002). Electronic fetal monitoring of the preterm fetus. *Journal of Perinatal and Neonatal Nursing, 16,* 12–24.

Bakker, P., Kurver, P. H., Kuik, D. J., & Van Geijn, H. P. (2007). Elevated uterine activity increases the risk of fetal acidosis at birth. *American Journal of Obstetrics and Gynecology, 196,* 313:e.1–6.

Blackburn, S. T. (2007). Pharmacology and pharmakinetics during the perinatal period. In *Maternal, fetal & neonatal physiology: A clinical perspective* (pp. 193–226). St. Louis, MO: Saunders.

Cahill, A. G., Waterman, B. M., Stamilio, D. M., Odibo, A. O., Allsworth, J. E., Evanoff, B., et al. (2008). Higher maximum doses of oxytocin are associated with an unacceptably high risk for uterine rupture in patients attempting vaginal birth after cesarean delivery. *American Journal of Obstetrics and Gynecology, 199*, 32:e1–e5.

Centers for Disease Control and Prevention. (2002). *Prevention of perinatal group B Streptococcal disease.* MMWR: Recommendations and Reports, 51, RR11. Available at http://www.cdc.gov/mmwr/preview/mmwrhtml/rr5111a1.htm Retrieved March 19, 2009.

Dauphinee, J. D. (2004). VBAC: Safety for the patient and the nurse. *Journal of Obstetric, Gynecologic, and Neonatal Nursing, 33*, 105–115.

Drakeley, A. J., Roberts, D., & Alfirevic, Z. (2003). Cervical stitch (cerclage) for preventing pregnancy loss in women. *Cochrane Database of Systematic Reviews, 1* (CD003253). DOI: 10.1002/14651858.CD003253.

Druzin, M. L., Smith, J. F., Gabbe, S. G., & Reed, K. L. (2007). Antepartum fetal evaluation. In S. G. Gabbe, J. R. Niebyl, & J. L. Simpson (Eds.), *Obstetrics: Normal and problem pregnancies,* (5th ed., pp. 267–300). Philadelphia: Churchill Livingstone.

Duff, P., Sweet, R. L., & Edwards, R. K. (2009). Maternal and fetal infections. In R. K. Creasy, R. Resnik, J. D. Iams, C. J. Lockwood, & T. R. Moore (Eds.), *Maternal-fetal medicine,* (6th ed., pp. 739–795). Philadelphia: Saunders.

Eganhouse, D. J., & Petersen, L. A. (1998). Fetal surveillance in multifetal pregnancy. *Journal of Obstetric, Gynecologic, and Neonatal Nursing, 27*, 312–321.

Ellings, J. M., Newman, R. B., & Bowers, N. A. (1998). Intrapartum care for women with multiple pregnancy. *Journal of Obstetric, Gynecologic, and Neonatal Nursing, 27*, 466–472.

Flamm, B. L. (2001). Vaginal birth after cesarean: Reducing medical and legal risks. *Clinical Obstetrics and Gynecology, 44*, 622–629.

Francois, K. E., & Foley, M. R. (2007). Antepartum and postpartum hemorrhage. In S. G. Gabbe, J. R. Niebyl, & J. L. Simpson (Eds.), *Obstetrics: Normal and problem pregnancies,* (5th ed., pp. 456–485). New York: Churchill Livingstone.

Freeman, R. K., Garite, T. J., & Nageotte, M. P. (2003). *Fetal heart rate monitoring,* (3rd ed.). Philadelphia: Lippincott Williams & Wilkins.

Froen, J. F., Heazell, A. E., Tveit, J. V., Saasted, E., Fretts, R. C., & Flenady, V. (2008). Fetal movement assessment. *Seminars in Perinatology, 32*, 243–246.

Garite, T. J. (2007). Intrapartum fetal evaluation. In S. G. Gabbe, J. R. Niebyl, J. L. Simpson, H. Galan, L. Goetzl, R. M. Eric Jauniaux, & M. Landon (Eds), *Obstetrics: Normal and problem pregnancies,* (5th ed., pp. 364–395). New York: Churchill Livingstone.

Garite, T. J., & Freeman, R. K. (1982). Chorioamnionitis in the preterm gestation. *Obstetrics & Gynecology, 59*, 539–545.

Gray, S. E., Rodis, J. F., Lettieri, L., Egan, J. F. X., & Vintzileos, A. (1994). Effect of intravenous magnesium sulfate on the biophysical profile of the healthy preterm fetus. *American Journal of Obstetricians and Gynecologists, 170*, 1131–1135.

Hall, D. (2009). Abruptio placentae and disseminated intravascular coagulopathy. *Seminars in Perinatology, 33*, 189–195.

Hallack, Mr., Martinez-Payer, J., Kruger, M., Hassan, S., Blackwell; & Sorokin, Y. (1999). The effect of magnesium sulfate on fetal heart rate parameters: A randomized, placebo-control trail. American Journal of Obstetrics and Gynecology. Volume 181, Issues p. 1122–1127.

Harjo, J. (1998). Diagnostic tests and laboratory values. In C. Kenner & J. Lott (Eds.), *Comprehensive neonatal nursing: A physiologic perspective* (2nd ed., p. 758). Philadelphia: Elsevier, Inc.

Hatjis, C. G., & Meis, P. J. (1986). Sinusoidal fetal heart rate pattern associated with butorphanol administration. *Obstetrics and Gynecology, 67*, 377–380.

Hawkins, J. L. (2005). Anesthesia for the pregnant patient undergoing nonobstetric surgery. *Refresher Courses in Anesthesiology, 33*, 137–144.

Hiett, A. K., Devoe, L. D., Brown, H. L., & Watson, J. (1995). Effect of magnesium on fetal heart rate variability using computer analysis. *American Journal of Perinatology, 12,* 259–261.

Hladky, K., Yankowitz, J., & Hansen, W. F. (2002). Placental abruption. *Obstetrical and Gynecological Survey, 57,* 299–305.

Iams, J. D. (2009). Cervical insufficiency. In R. K. Creasy, R. Resnik, J. D. Iams, C. J. Lockwood, & T. R. Moore (Eds.), *Creasy and Resnik's maternal-fetal medicine,* (6th ed., pp. 583–598). Philadelphia: Saunders.

Inturrisi, M. (2000). Perioperative assessment of fetal heart rate and uterine activity. *Journal of Obstetric, Gynecologic, and Neonatal Nursing, 29,* 331–336.

Kendrick, J. M. (1994). Fetal and uterine response during maternal surgery. *The American Journal of Maternal Child Nursing, 19,* 165–170.

Kendrick, J., Woodard, C. B., & Cross, S. B. (1995). Surveyed use of fetal and uterine monitoring during maternal surgery. *Journal of American Operating Room Nurse, 62,* 386–392.

Landon, M. B., Spong, C. Y., Thom, E., Hauth, J. C., Bloom, S. L., Varner, M. R., et al. (2006). Risk of uterine rupture with a trial of labor in women with multiple and single prior cesarean delivery. *Obstetrics and Gynecology, 108,* 12–20.

Leung, A. S., Leung, E. K., & Paul, R. H. (1993). Uterine rupture after previous cesarean delivery: Maternal and fetal consequences. *American Journal of Obstetrics and Gynecology, 169,* 945–950.

Macones, G. A., Hankins, G. D., Spong, C. Y., Hauth, J. D., & Moore, T. (2008). The 2008 National Institute of Child Health Human Development workshop report on electronic fetal monitoring: Update on definitions, interpretation, and research guidelines. *Obstetrics & Gynecology, 112,* 661–666; and *Journal of Obstetric, Gynecologic and Neonatal Nursing, 37,* 510–515.

Martin, J. A., Hamilton, B. E., Sutton, P. D., Ventura, S. J., Menacker, F., Dimeyer, S., et al. (2009). *Births: Final data for 2006.* National Vital Statistics Report 57.

Meis, P. J., Ureda, J. R., Swain, M., Kelly, R. T., Penry, M., & Sharp, P. (1986). Variable decelerations during nonstress tests are not a sign of fetal compromise. *American Journal of Obstetrics & Gynecology, 154,* 586–590.

Menihan, C. A. (1998). Uterine rupture in women attempting a vaginal birth following prior cesarean birth. *Journal of Perinatology, 18,* 440–443.

Mercer, B. M. (2009). Premature rupture of the membranes. In R. K. Creasy, R. Resnik, J. D. Iams, C. J. Lockwood, & T. R. Moore (Eds.), *Creasy and Resnik's maternal-fetal medicine,* (6th ed., pp. 599–626). Philadelphia: Saunders.

Modanlou, H., & Murata, Y. (2004). Sinusoidal heart rate pattern: Reappraisal of its definition and clinical significance. *Journal of Obstetrics and Gynaecology Research, 30,* 169–180.

Nageotte, M. P., & Gilstrap, L. C. (2009). Intrapartum fetal surveillance. In R. K. Creasy, R. Resnik, J. D. Iams, C. J. Lockwood, & T. R. Moore (Eds.), *Maternal-fetal medicine* (6th ed., pp. 398–417). Philadelphia: Saunders.

National Institutes of Health. (2000). National High Blood Pressure Education Program Working group on high blood pressure in pregnancy, NIH Publication No. 00-3029. Available at: http://www.nhlbi.nih.gov/guidelines/archives/hbp_preg/index.htm "Archive for historical reference only"

Newman, R. B., Gill, P. J., Campion, S., & Katz, M. (1987). Antepartum ambulatory tocodynamometry: The significance of low-amplitude, high-frequency contractions. *Obstetrics & Gynecology, 70,* 701–705.

O'Brien-Abel, N. (2003). Uterine rupture during VBAC trial of labor: Risk factors and fetal response. *Journal of Midwifery and Women's Health, 48,* 249–257.

Oyelese, Y., & Ananth, C. V. (2006). Placental abruption. *Obstetrics & Gynecology, 108,* 1005–1016.

Peaceman, A. M., Meyer, B. A., Thorp, J. A., Parisi, V. M., & Creasy, R. K. (1989). The effect of magnesium sulfate tocolysis on the fetal biophysical profile. *American Journal of Obstetrics & Gynecology, 161*, 771–774.

Porreco, R. P., Clark, S. L., Belfort, M. A., Dildy, G. A., & Myers, J. A. (2009). The changing specter of uterine rupture. *American Journal of Obstetrics and Gynecology, 200*, 269:e1–e4.

Porteous, J. (2008). Oh, by the way, the patient is pregnant! *Canadian Operating Room Nursing Journal, 26*, 35–42.

Ramsay, M. M., James, D. K., Steer, P. J., Weiner, C. P., & Gonik, B. (2000). *Normal values in pregnancy* (2nd ed.). New York: Saunders.

Roberts, J. M., & Funai, E. F. (2009). Pregnancy-related hypertension. In R. K. Creasy, R. Resnik, J. D. Iams, C. J. Lockwood, & T. R. Moore (Eds.), *Creasy and Resnik's maternal-fetal medicine* (6th ed., pp. 651–688). Philadelphia: Saunders.

Rosenberg, A. A. (2002). *The neonate. Obstetrics normal and problem pregnancies,* (5th ed., pp. 678–685). New York: Churchill Livingstone.

Shaver, S. M., & Shaver, D. C. (2005). Perioperative assessment of the obstetric patient undergoing abdominal surgery. *Journal of Perianesthesia Nursing, 20*, 160–166.

Sibai, B. M. (2007). Hypertension. In S. G. Gabbe, J. R. Niebyl, & J. L. Simpson (Eds.), *Obstetrics: Normal and problem pregnancies,* (5th ed., pp. 456–485). New York: Churchill Livingstone.

Simpson, K. R. (2004). Monitoring the preterm fetus during labor. *American Journal of Maternal Child Nursing, 29*, 380–388.

Society of Obstetricians and Gynaecologists of Canada. (2007). Fetal health surveillance: Antepartum and intrapartum consensus guidelines in (SOGC Clinical Practice Guidelines No. 197). *Journal of Obstetrics and Gynaecology in Canada, 29*, S3–S56.

Communication, Documentation, and Risk Management

American Academy of Pediatrics & American College of Obstetricians and Gynecologists. (2007). *Guidelines for perinatal care,* (6th ed.). Elk Grove Village, IL: Authors.

American College of Nurse Midwives. (2007). Intermittent auscultation for intrapartum fetal heart rate surveillance (Clinical Bulletin No. 9, March 2007). *Journal of Nurse Midwifery and Women's Health, 52*, 314–319.

Angelini, D., & Greenwald, L. (2005). Closed claim analysis of 65 medical malpractice cases involving nurse-midwives. *Journal of Midwifery and Women's Health, 50*, 454–460.

Association of Women's Health, Obstetric, and Neonatal Nurses. (2008). *Nursing management of the second stage of labor* (Evidence Based Clinical Practice Guideline). Washington, DC: Author.

Association of Women's Health, Obstetric, and Neonatal Nurses. (2009). *Fetal heart monitoring* (Position Statement). Washington, DC: Author.

Cady, R. F. (2003). *The advanced practice nurse's legal handbook.* Philadelphia: Lippincott.

Connelly, L. M., Yoder, L. H., & Miner-Williams, D. (2003). A qualitative study of charge nurse competencies. *Medical-Surgical Nursing, 12*, 298–305.

Daniel-Spiegel, E., Weiner, Z., Ben-Shiomo, I., & Shalev, E. (2004). For how long should oxytocin be continued during induction of labor? *British Journal of Obstetrics and Gynaecology, 111*, 331–334.

Edwards, C., & Woodard, E. K. (2008). SBAR for maternal transports: Going the extra mile. *Nursing for Women's Health, 12*, 515–520.

Elm, J. (2004). Improving labor and delivery shift report: Adapt this tool for your clinical setting to aid in patient care. *AWHONN Lifelines, 8*, 54–59.

Feinstein, N. F., Sprague, A., & Trepanier, M. J. (2008). *Fetal heart rate auscultation*, (2nd ed.). Washington, DC: Association of Women's Health, Obstetric, and Neonatal Nurses.

Fox, M., Kilpatrick, S., King, T., & Parer, J. (2000). Fetal heart rate monitoring: Interpretation and collaborative management. *Journal of Midwifery and Women's Health, 45*, 498–507.

Greenwald, L. M., & Mondor, M. (2003). Malpractice and the perinatal nurse. *Journal of Perinatal and Neonatal Nursing, 17*, 101–109.

Guise, J., & Lowe, N. (2006). Do you speak SBAR? *Journal of Obstetric, Gynecologic, and Neonatal Nursing, 35*, 313–314.

Haig, K. M., Sutton, S., & Whittington, J. (2006). SBAR: A shared mental model for improving communication between clinicians. *Joint Commission Journal on Quality and Patient Safety, 32*, 167–175.

Jevitt, C., Schuiling, K. D., & Summers, L. (2005). The national practitioner data bank: Information for and about midwifery. *Journal of Midwifery and Women's Health, 50*, 525–530.

Joint Commission on Accreditation of Healthcare Organizations (The Joint Commission). (2004). Preventing infant death during delivery (Sentinel Event Alert No. 30). Available at http://www.jointcommission.org/SentinelEvents/SentinelEventAlert/sea_30.htm Retrieved May 29, 2009.

Joint Commission on Accreditation of Healthcare Organizations (The Joint Commission). (2009). Sentinel events. Available at http://www.jointcommission.org/SentinelEvents/SentinelEventAlert Retrieved May 29, 2009.

King-Urbanski, T., & Cady, R. F. (1999). Documentation. In D. M. Rostant & R. F. Cady (Eds.), *Liability issues in perinatal nursing* (pp. 225–241). Philadelphia: Lippincott.

Krugman, M., & Smith, V. (2003). Charge nurse leadership development and evaluation. *Journal of Nursing Administration, 33*, 284–292.

Ladebauche, P. (1995). Limiting liability to avoid malpractice litigation. *The American Journal of Maternal Child Nursing, 20*, 243–248

Macones, G. A., Hankins, G. D., Spong, C. Y., Hauth, J. D., & Moore, T. (2008). The 2008 National Institute of Child Health Human Development workshop report on electronic fetal monitoring: Update on definitions, interpretations, and research guidelines. *Obstetrics & Gynecology, 112*, 661–666; and *Journal of Obstetric, Gynecologic and Neonatal Nursing, 37*, 510–515.

Mahlmeister, L. (1999). Professional accountability and legal liability for the team leader and charge nurse. *Journal of Obstetric, Gynecologic, and Neonatal Nursing, 28*, 300–309.

Mahlmeister, L. (2005). Preventing adverse perinatal outcomes through effective communication: Lessons learned. *Journal of Perinatal and Neonatal Nursing, 19*, 295–297.

Mahlmeister, L. (2006). Best practices in perinatal nursing: Professional role development for charge nurses. *Journal of Perinatal and Neonatal Nursing, 20*, 122–124.

McCaffrey, M. P., Neumann, D., Furniss, K. K., Lohman, S. L., Carpenito, P. M., & Johnson, V. L. (2008). The loneliness of the perinatal nurse in litigation. *The American Journal of Maternal Child Nursing, 33*, 281–286.

Miller, L. A. (2005). System errors in intrapartum electronic fetal monitoring: A case review. *Journal of Midwifery and Women's Health, 50*, 507–516.

Murphy, E. K. (2003). Withdrawing consent after a procedure has begun. *Association of Operating Room Nurses, 78*, 116–121.

National Institute of Child Health and Human Development Research Planning Workshop. (1997). Electronic fetal heart rate monitoring research guidelines for interpretation. *American Journal of Obstetrics and Gynecology, 177*, 1385–1390.

Patterson, E. S., Roth, E. M., Woods, D. D., Chow, R., & Orlando, J. (2004). Handoff strategies in settings with high consequences for failure: Lessons for health operations. *Internal Journal for Quality in Health Care, 16*, 125–132.

Simpson, K. R. (2004a). Second stage labor care. *The American Journal of Maternal Child Nursing, 29*, 416.

Simpson, K. R. (2004b). Standardized language for electronic fetal heart rate monitoring. *The American Journal of Maternal Child Nursing, 29*, 336.

Simpson, K. R. (2005). Handling handoffs safely. *The American Journal of Maternal Child Nursing, 30*, 152.

Simpson, K. R. (2007). Disruptive clinician behavior. *The American Journal of Maternal Child Nursing, 32*, 64.

Simpson, K. R. (2008a). *Cervical ripening and induction and augmentation of labor,* (3rd ed.). Washington, DC: Association of Women's Health, Obstetric, and Neonatal Nurses.

Simpson, K. R. (2008b). Labor and birth. In K. R. Simpson & P. A. Creehan (Eds.), *AWHONN perinatal nursing,* (3rd ed., pp. 300–398). Philadelphia: Lippincott Williams and Wilkins.

Simpson, K. R., & Knox, G. E. (2000). Risk management and electronic fetal monitoring: Decreasing risk of adverse outcomes and liability exposure. *Journal of Perinatal and Neonatal Nursing, 14*, 40–52.

Simpson, K. R., & Knox, G. E. (2003). Common areas of litigation related to care during labor and birth. *Journal of Perinatal and Neonatal Nursing, 17*, 110–125.

Society of Obstetricians and Gynaecologists of Canada. (2007). Fetal health surveillance: Antepartum and intrapartum consensus guidelines in (SOGC Clinical Practice Guidelines No. 197). *Journal of Obstetrics and Gynaecology in Canada, 29*, S3–S56.

Sullivan, C. A., & Bowden, M. A. (1999). Nurse-physician communication. In D. M. Rostant & R. F. Cady (Eds.), *Liability issues in perinatal nursing* (pp. 257–270). Philadelphia: Lippincott.

Theroux, R. (2006). How to bring evidence into your practice. *AWHONN Lifelines, 10*, 244–249.

Tucker, S. M., Miller, L. A., & Miller, D. A. (2009). *Fetal monitoring: A multidisciplinary approach.* St. Louis: Mosby.

Woods, J. R., & Rozovsky, F. A. (2003). *What do I say? Communicating intended or unanticipated outcomes in obstetrics.* San Francisco: Jossey-Bass.

Membership Application

AWHONN
Association of Women's Health,
Obstetric and Neonatal Nurses

RECRUITED BY (IF APPLICABLE): _____   RECRUITER'S MEMBER #: _____

MEMBERSHIP CATEGORIES (CHOOSE ONE)

☐ Full $168	☐ Non-RN $144	☐ Student $84	☐ Retired $84	☐ International $192
RNs licensed in the US, its territories or Canada. May hold elected and appointed offices and may vote.	LPNs, LVNs or others interested in the health of women and newborns. May hold appointed office, but may not vote.	Eligible for 4 years. RNs may vote. Proof of current enrollment required. Please attach.	Must be at least 62 and no longer working as a nurse. Min. 3 years previous full membership required. RNs may vote.	A nurse or other interested party residing outside the US (other than members of the US Armed Forces). RNs may vote.

PREFIX (MS, MR, ETC.)   FIRST _____   MI _____   LAST _____   SUFFIX (JR., III, ETC.) _____

CREDENTIALS (RN, CNM, ETC.) _____   TITLE/POSITION (E.G., NURSE MANAGER, MIDWIFE, DIRECTOR, ETC.) _____

HOME ADDRESS _____   CITY _____   STATE/PROVINCE _____

ZIP/POSTAL CODE _____   COUNTRY _____   HOME PHONE _____

EMPLOYER _____   WORK ADDRESS _____   CITY _____   STATE/PROVINCE _____   ZIP/POSTAL CODE _____

WORK PHONE _____   WORK FAX _____

PREFERRED E-MAIL ADDRESS FOR AWHONN COMMUNICATION _____

PREFERRED MAILING ADDRESS (CHECK ONE)   ☐ WORK   ☐ HOME

☐ I AM CURRENTLY AN ACTIVE DUTY MEMBER OF THE US ARMED FORCES. BRANCH OF SERVICE (CHECK ONE)   ☐ ARMY   ☐ NAVY   ☐ AIR FORCE
(ACTIVE DUTY MEMBERS OF THE US ARMED FORCES WILL BE MEMBERS OF THE AWHONN ARMED FORCES SECTION.)
RANK : _____

☐ I AM AFFILIATED WITH THE US ARMED FORCES (RETIRED, RESERVIST, DOD CIVILIAN, ETC.) BUT AM NOT ON ACTIVE DUTY, AND I WOULD LIKE TO BE A MEMBER
OF THE AWHONN ARMED FORCES SECTION INSTEAD OF THE SECTION IN WHICH I RESIDE.

WE OCCASIONALLY MAKE OUR MAILING LIST AVAILABLE TO CAREFULLY SCREENED ORGANIZATIONS THAT OFFER PRODUCTS AND/OR SERVICES THAT MAY BE OF
INTEREST TO YOU. ☐ CHECK THIS BOX ONLY IF YOU DO NOT WANT TO RECEIVE SUCH MAILINGS.

METHOD OF PAYMENT*

☐ CHECK OR MONEY ORDER PAYABLE TO AWHONN

☐ VISA   ☐ MASTERCARD   ☐ AMERICAN EXPRESS

CARD NO _____   EXP DATE _____

CARD HOLDER'S NAME _____

SIGNATURE _____

*DUES SUBJECT TO CHANGE. MEMBERSHIP DUES ARE NOT REFUNDABLE.

AMOUNT ENCLOSED

DUES _____ $ _____

☐ OPTIONAL TAX-DEDUCTIBLE DONATION TO AWHONN   HEALTH FUNDS $30.00

TOTAL ENCLOSED _____ $ _____

ENTER PROMOTION CODE HERE, IF ANY _____

SUBMIT APPLICATION AND PAYMENT TO:
AWHONN, Dept. 4015, Washington, DC 20042-4015
Phone: 800-673-8499; 800-245-0231 (Canada)
Fax: 202-728-0575; www.awhonn.org

Member Profile

We want to make sure that we offer the professional nursing programs, services and products that are of greatest value to you. Please complete this member profile. Your answers will be kept confidential.

IN NURSING PRACTICE SINCE

_____

YEAR ONLY

DATE OF BIRTH

_____

DAY MO YR

GENDER: ☐ M ☐ F

PRIMARY POSITION (SELECT NO MORE THAN 2)
☐ CASE MANAGER
☐ CLINICAL NURSE SPECIALIST
☐ CONSULTANT
☐ FACULTY-ACADEMIC
☐ NURSE EXECUTIVE
☐ NURSE MANAGER/COORDINATOR
☐ NURSE MIDWIFE
☐ NURSE PRACTITIONER
☐ RESEARCHER
☐ STAFF DEVELOPMENT
☐ STAFF NURSE
☐ STUDENT
☐ OTHER:

ETHNIC/RACIAL BACKGROUND (SELECT ONE)
☐ AMERICAN INDIAN/ALASKA NATIVE
☐ ASIAN OR PACIFIC ISLANDER
☐ AFRICAN AMERICAN (NON-HISPANIC)
☐ HISPANIC
☐ WHITE (NON-HISPANIC)
☐ MULTIRACIAL

CERTIFICATIONS (CHECK ALL THAT APPLY)
☐ AMBULATORY WOMEN'S HEALTH
☐ CHILDBIRTH EDUCATOR
☐ EFM/FHM
☐ HIGH-RISK OB NURSING
☐ INPATIENT OB
☐ LACTATION CONSULTANT/EDUCATOR
☐ LOW-RISK NEONATAL NURSING
☐ MATERNAL NEWBORN NURSING
☐ NICU NURSING
☐ NEONATAL NURSE PRACTITIONER
☐ NURSING ADMINISTRATION
☐ NURSE MIDWIFE
☐ OB/GYN PRACTITIONER
☐ PERINATAL NURSE PRACTITIONER
☐ PERINATAL NURSING
☐ WOMEN'S HEALTH NURSE PRACTIONER
☐ OTHER:

HIGHEST DEGREE EARNED
☐ DOCTORATE
☐ MASTER'S
☐ BACHELOR'S
☐ ASSOCIATE
☐ DIPLOMA
☐ VOC-TECH
☐ OTHER:

MEDICATIONS AND/OR OTC PRODUCTS (CHECK ALL THAT APPLY)
☐ HAVE PRESCRIPTIVE AUTHORITY
☐ RECOMMEND MEDICATION AND/OR OTC PRODUCTS
☐ COUNSEL AND EDUCATE PATIENTS REGARDING USE OF MEDICATIONS AND/OR OTC PRODUCTS
☐ NO ROLE REGARDING MEDICATIONS AND/OR OTC PRODUCTS

EQUIPMENT AND SUPPLIES (CHECK ALL THAT APPLY)
☐ MAKE PURCHASING DECISIONS DIRECTLY
☐ RECOMMEND OR INFLUENCE DECISIONS
☐ NO ROLE REGARDING PURCHASE OF EQUIPMENT AND/OR SUPPLIES

PRIMARY CLINICAL FOCUS (SELECT NO MORE THAN 2)
☐ ANTEPARTUM
☐ BREASTFEEDING/LACTATION
☐ INTRAPARTUM (INCLUDES LDR/LDRP & L&D)
☐ NICU
☐ NURSERY
☐ WOMEN'S HEALTH
☐ POSTPARTUM (INCLUDES MOTHER-BABY)
☐ OTHER: _____

JOB SETTING
☐ ACADEMIA
☐ AMBULATORY CARE (INCLUDES PHYSICIAN OFFICE, OUTPATIENT CLINIC, ETC.)
☐ HOME HEALTH CARE
☐ HOSPITAL INPATIENT
☐ NOT WORKING
☐ PUBLIC HEALTH
☐ SELF-EMPLOYED
☐ OTHER:

MAJORITY OF TIME SPENT (SELECT NO MORE THAN 2)
☐ ADMINISTRATION
☐ CONSULTING
☐ DIRECT PATIENT CARE
☐ MANAGEMENT/SUPERVISION
☐ PATIENT EDUCATION
☐ RESEARCH
☐ STAFF DEVELOPMENT/EDUCATION
☐ UNDERGRAD/GRADUATE NURSING EDUCATION
☐ OTHER: _____

IS CONTINUING EDUCATION (CE) REQUIRED FOR YOU TO MAINTAIN LICENSURE AND/OR CERTIFICATION?
☐ YES   ☐ NO

OTHER MEMBERSHIPS
☐ AACN (CRITICAL CARE NURSES) AANP ACNM ANA
☐ ANN AONE NANN NPWH SIGMA THETA TAU
☐ OTHER: _____

HOW DID YOU LEARN ABOUT AWHONN?
☐ COLLEAGUE
☐ ADVERTISEMENT
☐ MAILING
☐ CONFERENCE/CONVENTION
☐ OTHER: _____

SUBMIT APPLICATION AND PAYMENT TO:
AWHONN, Dept. 4015, Washington, DC 20042-4015
Phone: 800-673-8499; 800-245-0231 (Canada)
Fax: 202-728-0575; www.awhonn.org

ADVANCED FETAL MONITORING COURSE TEST B ANSWER SHEET

Participant Name: _____

Date of Course: _____

Course Number: _____

Test B is to be administered only if the participant does not successfully complete Test A. If the participant successfully completes Test B, Competence Validation will be awarded. If the participants fail both Test A and Test B, Competence Validation should not be awarded.

**The corresponding original questions should be retained by the instructor.
This form should not be mailed back to the AWHONN processing center.**

Answer Sheet

	A	B	C		A	B	C		A	B	C		A	B	C		A	B	C
1	○	○	○	11	○	○	○	21	○	○	○	31	○	○	○	41	○	○	○
2	○	○	○	12	○	○	○	22	○	○	○	32	○	○	○	42	○	○	○
3	○	○	○	13	○	○	○	23	○	○	○	33	○	○	○	43	○	○	○
4	○	○	○	14	○	○	○	24	○	○	○	34	○	○	○	44	○	○	○
5	○	○	○	15	○	○	○	25	○	○	○	35	○	○	○	45	○	○	○
6	○	○	○	16	○	○	○	26	○	○	○	36	○	○	○	46	○	○	○
7	○	○	○	17	○	○	○	27	○	○	○	37	○	○	○	47	○	○	○
8	○	○	○	18	○	○	○	28	○	○	○	38	○	○	○	48	○	○	○
9	○	○	○	19	○	○	○	29	○	○	○	39	○	○	○	49	○	○	○
10	○	○	○	20	○	○	○	30	○	○	○	40	○	○	○	50	○	○	○

COURSE OUTLINE

AWHONN Advanced Fetal Monitoring Course

Disclosure

The Instructors of this course report either conflicts of interest or relevant financial relationships, or lack thereof.

The nurse planners for this course report no conflicts of interest.

Disclosure

The Instructors will be discussing an off-label use of the medication terbutaline but will not be discussing the off-label use of any medical devices.

© 2010 AWHONN 3

Course Objectives

1. Describe physiologic principles of maternal and fetal oxygen transfer and acid-base balance.
2. Identify physiologic principles underlying fetal heart monitoring.
3. Describe concepts in antenatal testing including analysis and interpretation of biophysical profiles and complex antenatal fetal heart monitoring tracings.
4. Relate physiologic principles to the goals and interventions of antenatal testing.
5. Evaluate interventions for patients undergoing antenatal testing.

© 2010 AWHONN 4

Course Objectives (cont.)

6. Analyze fetal cardiac arrhythmia patterns and describe outcomes associated with these patterns.

7. Analyze complex fetal heart monitoring patterns utilizing current NICHD/ACOG FHM terminology and categories.

8. Apply perinatal risk management principles, communication techniques and documentation strategies related to complex and challenging patient care scenarios.

© 2010 AWHONN 5

Fetal Oxygenation

- Maternal circulation
- Uterine circulation
- Placental circulation
- Umbilical circulation
- Fetus

© 2010 AWHONN 6

Maternal Transfer of Oxygen to Fetus

Transport from atmosphere to alveoli
↓
Diffusion across alveolar membrane
↓
Transport from lungs to placenta
↓
Diffusion across the placenta
↓
Transport from placenta to fetus
↓
Diffusion into fetal tissues

Adapted from Meschia, G. (1979). Supply of oxygen to the fetus. *J Reproductive Medicine, 23*, 160.

© 2010 AWHONN 7

Four Components of Oxygen Transport

- Oxygen content

- Oxygen affinity

- Oxygen delivery

- Oxygen consumption

© 2010 AWHONN 8

Maternal Oxygen Transport

Maternal oxygen content:

- The total amount of oxygen in the maternal arterial blood
  - Amount of oxygen dissolved in plasma (PaO_2)
  - Percent of oxygen carried on the hemoglobin (SaO_2)

© 2010 AWHONN 9

anemia ?   (4 molecules O_2 to one heme)

Maternal Oxygen Transport (cont.)

- PaO_2 helps bind oxygen molecules to hemoglobin.

- Saturated hemoglobin molecule carries four molecules of oxygen.

- SaO_2 is a more precise measure of oxygen content than PaO_2.

© 2010 AWHONN 10

Maternal Oxygen Transport (cont.)

Oxygen affinity:

- Gain and release of oxygen molecules from hemoglobin

- Can change with variations in pH, CO_2 or maternal temperature

- Reflected on oxyhemoglobin dissociation curve

© 2010 AWHONN 11

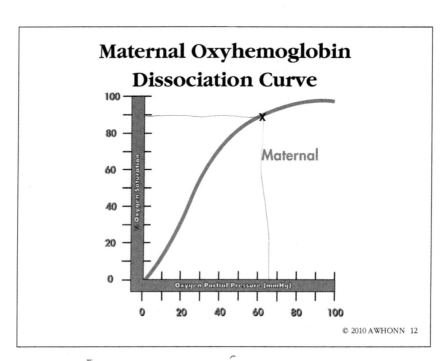

Maternal Oxyhemoglobin Dissociation Curve

© 2010 AWHONN 12

shift to Ⓒ ↑ affinity
   alkolosis, hypothermia
shift to Ⓚ ↓ affinity
   acidosis, fever, pregnancy

Maternal Oxygen Transport (cont.)

Oxygen delivery:
- Amount of oxygen delivered to the tissues each minute
- Two components are:
  - Oxygen content
  - Cardiac output

© 2010 AWHONN 13

Maternal Oxygen Transport (cont.)

Oxygen consumption:

Amount of oxygen consumed by the body and tissues each minute

© 2010 AWHONN 14

Nervous? Scared?
Working hard, Fever,
stress, labor
pain + anxiety

Interventions to Decrease Maternal Oxygen Consumption

- Promote maternal relaxation
- Coach with helpful breathing techniques
- Manage pain
- Maintain acceptable uterine activity (in some cases decreasing uterine activity)
- Use antipyretics to reduce fever
- Reposition the mother
- Provide appropriate management of second stage labor

© 2010 AWHONN 15

push with every other ctx.

Fetal Oxygen Transport

- Includes oxygen content, affinity, delivery and consumption
- Is directly dependent on maternal oxygen transport
- Is affected by:
  - Blood flow to the uterus and placenta
  - Integrity of the placenta
  - Blood flow through the umbilical cord

© 2010 AWHONN 16

Fetal Oxygen Transport (cont.)

Fetal oxygen content:

- Amount of oxygen dissolved in plasma (PaO_2)
- Amount of oxygen carried on the hemoglobin (SaO_2)
- Fetal PaO_2 is approximately 30 mmHg
  - Adult is 100 mmHg

© 2010 AWHONN 17

_____

_____

_____

_____

Fetal Oxygen Transport (cont.)

- Fetal oxygen tension is about 25% of an adult's
- Fetal hemoglobin:
  - Has an increased oxygen affinity
  - Has a higher concentration than maternal (approximately 17 gm/dL at term)

(Freeman et al., 2003; Harvey & Chez, 1997)

© 2010 AWHONN 18

_____

_____

_____

_____

Fetal Oxygen Transport (cont.)

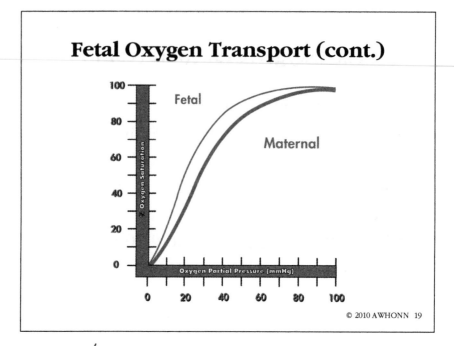

© 2010 AWHONN 19

fetal – left shift

O_2 attatches more easy to hemoglobin

Fetal Circulation

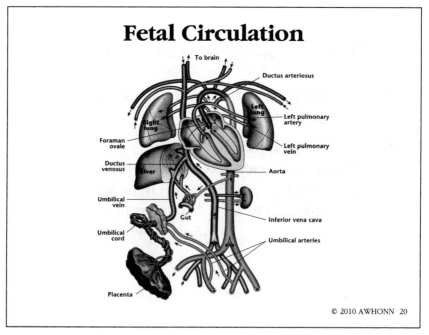

© 2010 AWHONN 20

heart + brain, most O_2 needs

Fetal Oxygen Transport (cont.)

- Fetal oxygen consumption:
  - Amount of oxygen consumed by the tissues each minute
- Fetal response to decreased oxygen consumption:
  - Alteration in behavioral state
    - Decreased fetal movement
  - Change in variability
  - Change in reactivity

© 2010 AWHONN 21

Is your baby moving?

Fetal Response to Decreased Oxygen

- Redistribution of blood to vital organs

- Oxygen consumption decreases:
  - Myocardium uses less oxygen
  - Changes in FHR

- Aerobic to anaerobic metabolism

© 2010 AWHONN 22

↓ variability, decels

Aerobic versus Anaerobic Metabolism

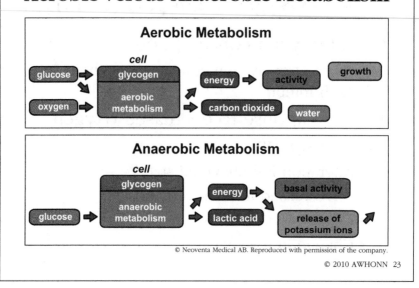

Aerobic Metabolism

cell

glucose → glycogen → energy → activity → growth

oxygen → aerobic metabolism → carbon dioxide → water

Anaerobic Metabolism

cell

glucose → glycogen / anaerobic metabolism → energy → basal activity

→ lactic acid → release of potassium ions

© Neoventa Medical AB. Reproduced with permission of the company.

© 2010 AWHONN 23

Technology for Analysis of Fetal Hypoxia

- Fetal ECG analysis

- ST-segment analysis

© 2010 AWHONN 24

Definitions of Key Terms

- Base deficit: HCO_3 concentration lower than normal

- Base excess: HCO_3 concentration higher than normal

- Acidemia: ↑concentration of hydrogen ions in the
 blood

- Acidosis: ↑concentration of hydrogen ions in the
 tissue

© 2010 AWHONN 25

Definitions of Key Terms (cont.)

- Hypoxemia: ↓ oxygen content in the blood

- Hypoxia: ↓ level of oxygen in the tissue

- Asphyxia: hypoxia, acidemia and metabolic
 acidosis

⤷ *sentinel events*

© 2010 AWHONN 26

Neonatal Encephalopathy and Cerebral Palsy

Neonatal encephalopathy:

- "A clinically defined syndrome of disturbed neurologic function in the earliest days of life in the term infant, manifested by difficulty with initiating and maintaining respiration, depression of tone and reflexes, subnormal level of consciousness, and often by seizures"

(ACOG, 2003, p. 84)

© 2010 AWHONN 27

Neonatal Encephalopathy and Cerebral Palsy (cont.)

Four criteria define an acute intrapartum event sufficient to cause cerebral palsy (ACOG, 2003 p. xviii):

- Evidence of metabolic acidosis in fetal umbilical arterial blood obtained at delivery (pH <7 and base deficit ≥12 mmol/L)

© 2010 AWHONN 28

Neonatal Encephalopathy and Cerebral Palsy (cont.)

Criteria continued:

- Early onset of severe or moderate neonatal encephalopathy in infants born at 34 or more weeks of gestation

(ACOG, 2003)

© 2010 AWHONN 29

Neonatal Encephalopathy and Cerebral Palsy (cont.)

Criteria continued:

- Cerebral palsy of spastic quadriplegic or dyskinetic type

(ACOG, 2003)

→ only intrapartum type

© 2010 AWHONN 30

neurologic disorders
parts of brain that control movement.

Types of Cerebral Palsy (CP)

Spastic Cerebral Palsy

- Impacts 70–80% of individuals with CP

- Characterized by stiff muscles

- Spastic quadriplegia, the most severe form, is associated with mental retardation

© 2010 AWHONN 31

Types of Cerebral Palsy (cont.)

Athetoid/Dyskinetic

- Impacts 10–20% of individuals with CP

- Characterized by fluctuations in muscle tone and uncontrolled movement

- Associated with sucking, swallowing, and speech impediments

© 2010 AWHONN 32

#4

Neonatal Encephalopathy and Cerebral Palsy (cont.)

Criteria continued:

- Exclusion of other identifiable etiologies such as trauma, coagulation disorders, infectious conditions or genetic disorders

(ACOG, 2003)

© 2010 AWHONN 33

_____ original _____ intent FHM _____
_____
_____
_____

Absence of Metabolic Acidemia

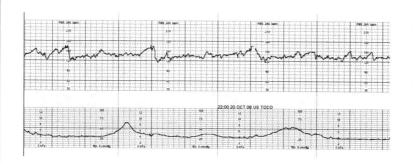

© 2010 AWHONN 34

_____ acidemia develops over 1 hr _____
_____ subtle changes _____
_____
_____

Systematic Assessment of FHR Tracings

- Baseline rate
- Variability
- Periodic/episodic changes
- Uterine activity
- Pattern evolution
- Accompanying clinical characteristics
- Urgency

Adapted from Fox, Kilpatrick, King, & Parer (2000)

© 2010 AWHONN 35

NICHD FHR Interpretation System

Normal
Fetal Acid-Base Status:
Well-Oxygenated Fetus

All of the following:
- Baseline rate: 110–160 bpm
- Baseline variability: moderate
- Late or variable decelerations: absent
- Early decelerations: present or absent
- Accelerations: present or absent

Indeterminate:
Compensatory
Response

Examples:
- Moderate variability with recurrent late or variable decelerations
- Minimal variability with recurrent variable decelerations
- Absent variability without recurrent decelerations
- Bradycardia with moderate variability
- Prolonged decelerations
- Tachycardia

Abnormal Fetal Acid-Base Status

Category I   *Category II*   *Category III*

© 2010 AWHONN 36

Management Strategies

- Tracings may evolve between categories
- Category I:
  - Followed in routine manner
- Category II:
  - Requires evaluation, continued surveillance and interventions guided by the clinical picture
- Category III:
  - Requires prompt evaluation
  - Use interventions

© 2010 AWHONN 37

Systematic Decision Making

- Includes:
  - Intrapartum goals
  - Ongoing assessment
  - Physiologic interventions
  - Clinical evaluation

© 2010 AWHONN 38

JoAnn, 17 Years Old, $G_1 P_0$, 40 5/7 Weeks' Gestation

- Family history: none provided
- Medical history:
  - Car accident one year ago; broken arm and facial lacerations
- Previous pregnancies: denies
- Psychosocial history:
  - In an abusive relationship
  - Not in school
  - Not living with parents

© 2010 AWHONN 39

alcohol + cocaine 1st tri
2-3 cup day
⊕ EI ,

JoAnn (cont.): Current Pregnancy

- Four prenatal visits; two different providers

- First trimester substance abuse

- Current tobacco use

- Normal prenatal lab values

© 2010 AWHONN 40

JoAnn (cont.): Admission Data

- SROM 0655:
  - Large amount of pooling clear fluid
  - Fern positive

- SVE: 1–2/80%/ -1; cephalic presentation

- VS: BP 119/73, P 75, R 20, afebrile

JoAnn (cont.): 1005

US/TOCO

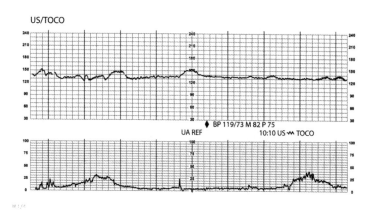

BP 119/73 M 82 P 75

UA REF   10:10 US ⋏ TOCO

JoAnn (cont.): 1640

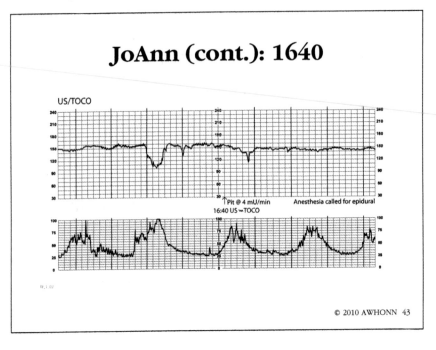

US/TOCO

↑Pit @ 4 mU/min   Anesthesia called for epidural
16:40 US ~TOCO

© 2010 AWHONN 43

JoAnn (cont.): 1640

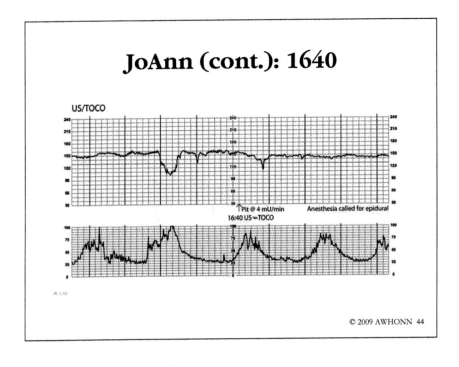

US/TOCO

↑Pit @ 4 mU/min   Anesthesia called for epidural
16:40 US ~TOCO

© 2009 AWHONN 44

JoAnn (cont.): 1715

US/TOCO

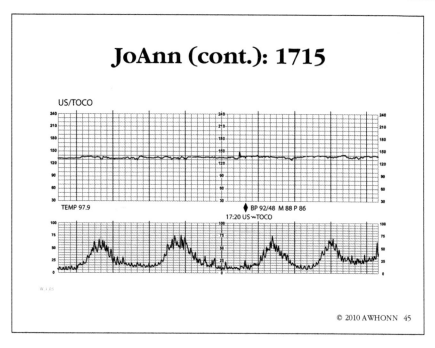

TEMP 97.9   ◆ BP 92/48 M 88 P 86
17:20 US ⁓TOCO

© 2010 AWHONN 45

Effects of Ephedrine

- Maternal:
  - ↑ Cardiac output
  - ↑ Heart rate
  - ↑ Blood pressure
- Fetal:
  - Tachycardia
  - ↑ FHR variability
  - ↑ accelerations

© 2010 AWHONN 46

JoAnn (cont.): 1800

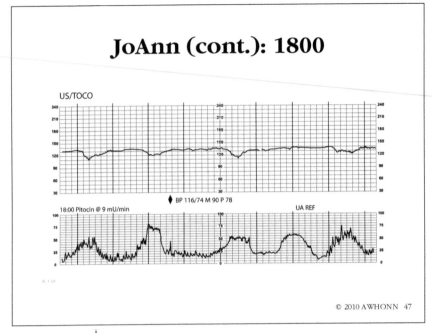

US/TOCO

BP 116/74 M 90 P 78

18:00 Pitocin @ 9 mU/min   UA REF

4/90/-1   cat II
early, min var.

1846

P

JoAnn (cont.): 1925

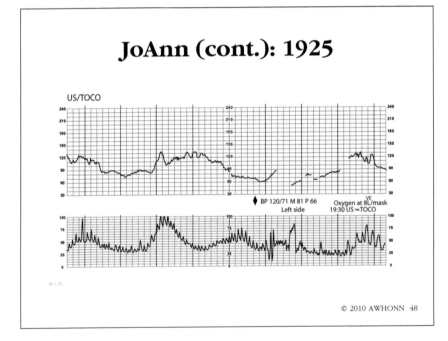

US/TOCO

BP 120/71 M 81 P 66
Left side

VE
Oxygen at 8L/mask
19:30 US ~ TOCO

pit ↓ 6

JoAnn (cont.): 1938

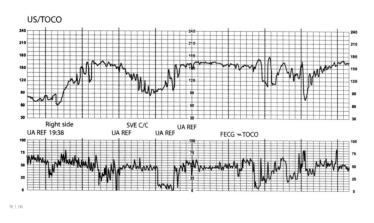

US/TOCO

Right side
UA REF 19:38   SVE C/C   UA REF
                      UA REF   UA REF   FECG TOCO

© 2010 AWHONN 49

JoAnn (cont.): Outcome

- Cesarean birth with epidural anesthesia
- Male infant, 6 lb, 7 oz (2,920 grams)
- Apgar scores 1/ 6/ 7
- Moderate clot in uterine cavity, partial abruption
- Very thin nuchal cord ×2
- Grade III placenta with calcification

© 2010 AWHONN 50

The Physiologic Basis for Advanced Fetal Heart Monitoring

- Physiologic principles underlying fetal heart monitoring
- Advanced physiologic principles of maternal and fetal oxygen transfer and acid-base balance
- Clinical decision making when utilizing fetal heart monitoring

© 2010 AWHONN 51

_____

_____

_____

_____

Antepartum Fetal Assessment

© 2010 AWHONN 52

Indications for Antenatal Testing

- Decreased uteroplacental blood flow (IUGR)
- Decreased gas exchange (placental abruption)
- Abnormal metabolic processes (diabetes)
- Fetal infection (cytomegalovirus)
- Fetal anemia (maternal-fetal hemorrhage)
- Abnormal fetal cardiac issues (anomalies, arrhythmia)
- Umbilical cord accident candidates (oligohydramnios)

© 2010 AWHONN 53

Fetal Response to Hypoxemia

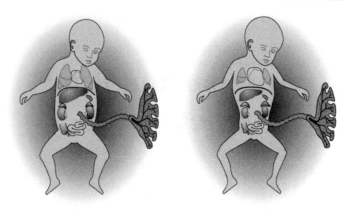

Normoxia   Hypoxia

© 2010 AWHONN 54

_____

_____

_____

_____

Risk of Fetal Compromise

- Increased fetal cardiac output
- Doppler flow changes:
  - Increased S/D ratios ➔ absent and reversed flow
- Declining levels of amniotic fluid
- Abnormal biophysical profile characteristics
- Abnormal FHR characteristics

© 2010 AWHONN 55

_____

_____

_____

_____

Methods of Antepartum Fetal Testing

- Fetal movement counts (FMC)
- Nonstress test (NST)
- Vibroacoustic stimulation (VAS)
- Contraction stress test (CST)
- Oxytocin challenge test (OCT)
- Biophysical profile (BPP)
- Modified biophysical profile
- Doppler flow studies

© 2010 AWHONN 56

Fetal Movement Counts (FMC)

- Perception of fetal movement by the woman
- Decreased fetal movement in response to hypoxemia
- Variety of FMC methods because ideal number of movements and optimal counting duration have not been defined

© 2010 AWHONN 57

 # movements over time
reduce stillbirth rate.

Factors Influencing Fetal Movement

- Diurnal variations
- Gestational age
- Tobacco
- Medications
  - Steroids
  - Narcotics
- Food or liquid intake

© 2010 AWHONN 58

Nonstress Test

- Primary antepartum assessment tool

- External assessment of:
  - Fetal heart rate
  - Oxygenation
  - Neurologic function
  - Cardiac function

© 2010 AWHONN 59

NST Interpretation

- Reactive:
  - ≥2 FHR accelerations ≥15 bpm above BL, lasting ≥15 seconds within 20 minutes; may extend the time to 40 minutes

- Nonreactive:
  - No FHR accelerations meeting criteria within a maximum of 40 minutes

© 2010 AWHONN 60

50% non reactive 24-28 wks

NST Interpretation: Fetus Less than 32 Weeks' Gestation

Reactive:

- ≥2 FHR accelerations ≥10 bpm above BL, lasting ≥10 seconds within 20 minutes; may extend testing time to 60–90 minutes

Nonreactive:

- No FHR accelerations meeting criteria within a maximum of 90 minutes

© 2010 AWHONN 61

Nonstress Test

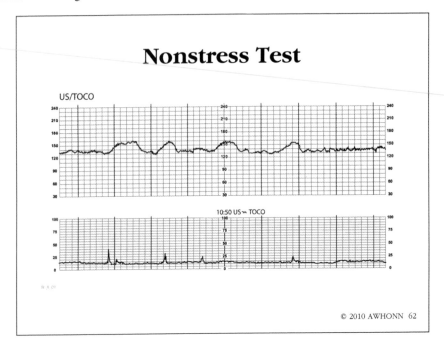

US/TOCO

10:50 US ⁓ TOCO

_____

_____

_____

_____

Nonstress Test

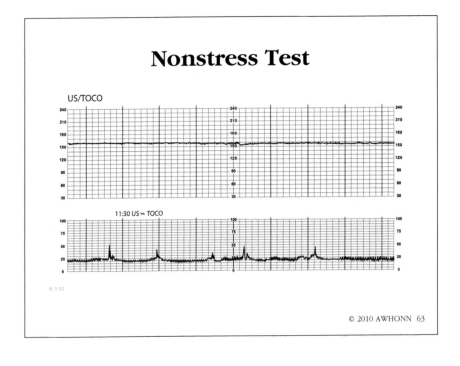

US/TOCO

11:30 US ⁓ TOCO

_____

_____

_____

_____

Variable Decelerations and NST

- Variable decelerations may occur during the NST

- Nonrepetitive lasting <30 seconds

- Repetitive (three or more in 20 minutes)

- Consider amniotic fluid index

© 2010 AWHONN 64

_____

_____

_____

_____

Vibroacoustic Stimulation (VAS)

- Vibroacoustic stimulation (VAS):
  - Evaluation of FHR response to acoustic stimulation
  - Establish baseline
  - Apply up to a three-second stimulus near the fetal head
  - May repeat every minute up to three times
- Two or more accelerations in a 20-minute period after stimulus

© 2010 AWHONN 65

_____

_____

_____

_____

VAS (cont.)

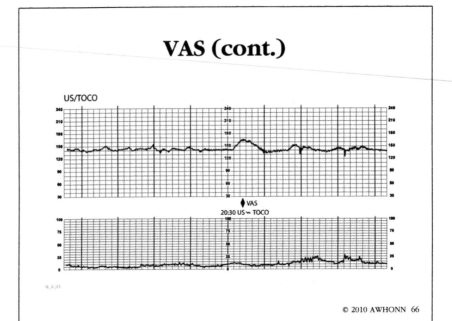

US/TOCO

♦ VAS
20:30 US ⁓ TOCO

© 2010 AWHONN 66

Contraction Stress Test

- Also called oxytocin challenge test

- Fetal heart responses to uterine contractions

© 2010 AWHONN 67

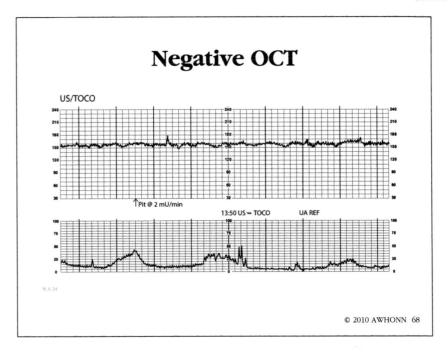

Negative OCT

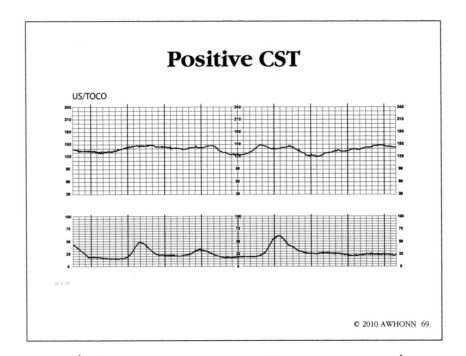

Positive CST

late decels c̄ > 50% CTX even if
CTX freq < 2-3 min

Equivocal-Suspicious CST

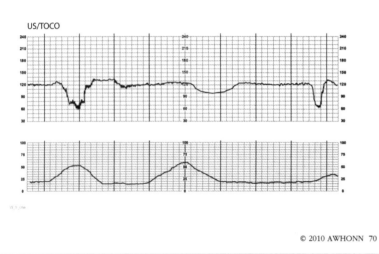

US/TOCO

intermittent late

Equivocal-Hyperstimulation OCT
(Tachysystole)

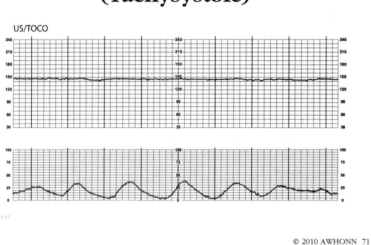

US/TOCO

hyperstim

Unsatisfactory CST

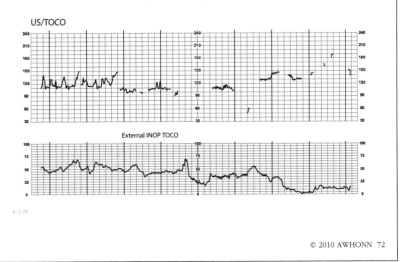

US/TOCO

External INOP TOCO

© 2010 AWHONN 72

not good tracing

Biophysical Profile (BPP)

- Combination of <u>NST</u> and four ᘔ
  ultrasound biophysical characteristics:
  - Fetal <u>movement</u> ᘔ
  - Fetal <u>tone</u> ᘔ
  - Fetal <u>breathing</u> ᘔ
  - Amniotic fluid volume ᘔ

© 2010 AWHONN 73

over 30 minutes

BPP Interpretation

Parameter	Normal (2)	Abnormal (0)
Reactive FHR	At least two episodes of FHR acceleration of 15 × 15 with FM in 30 minutes	< Two episodes of acceleration of FHR or acceleration <15 bpm in 30 minutes
Fetal breathing	At least one episode of fetal breathing movement (FBM) of at least 30 seconds within 30 minutes	Absent FBM or no episode of ≥ 30 seconds in 30 minutes
Gross body movement	At least three discrete body/ limb movements in 30 minutes (active continuous movement episode equals a single movement)	≤ Two episodes of body/limb movements in 30 minutes

© 2010 AWHONN 74

BPP Interpretation (cont.)

Parameter	Normal (2)	Abnormal (0)
Fetal tone	At least one episode of active extension with return to flexion of fetal limbs or trunk. opening and closing of hand equals normal tone	Slow extension, return to partial flexion; or movement of limb in full extension; or absent FM with fetal hand in complete or partial deflection
Qualitative AFV	At least one pocket of amniotic fluid (AF) that measures at least 2 cm in two perpendicular planes	No AF pockets; or pocket < 2 cm in two perpendicular planes

© 2010 AWHONN 75

Hand Extension and Flexion

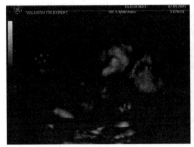

Images used with permission of GE Healthcare

© 2010 AWHONN 76

Biophysical Profile Interpretation

- Normal BPP score:
    - 8–10 indicative of fetal oxygenation
- Score of 6 or less:
    - Abnormal score
    - Associated with abnormal cord pH
    - Indicative of diminished blood flow through uteroplacental unit

© 2010 AWHONN 77

Interpretation and Suggested Management for BPP

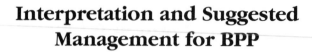

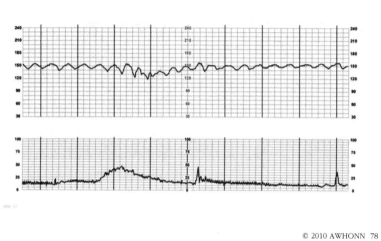

© 2010 AWHONN 78

Chronic asphyxia
fetal anemia

Modified BPP

NST and Amniotic
Fluid Index (AFI)

- Largest vertical
  pocket in four
  quadrants
- AFI is the total of
  four quadrants

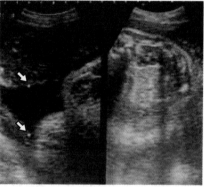

Used with permission from GE Healthcare

© 2010 AWHONN 79

Doppler Flow Studies

- Blood flow velocity studied
- Measures components of cardiac cycle
- Flow through arteries:
  - Uterine
  - Umbilical
  - Middle cerebral

© 2010 AWHONN 80

_____

_____

_____

_____

Interpretation

- Normal flow

- Absent end diastolic flow

- Reverse end diastolic flow

Used with permission from GE Healthcare

© 2010 AWHONN 81

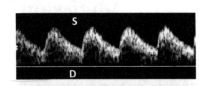

umbilical artery
or
cerebral artery

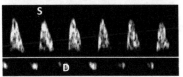

— terminal
death
soon
(sock flow)

_____ The placenta is unable to
supply fetus's needs _____

_____

_____

Margaret, 30 Years Old
$G_2 P_{1001}$, 32 2/7 Weeks' Gestation

- Family history: unremarkable
- Medical/surgical history: unremarkable
- Pregnancy history:
  - SVD at 37 weeks for preeclampsia
  - PUPPS during third trimester
  - Viable male infant, 6 lb, 13 oz
- Current pregnancy
  - Abnormal second trimester screening test
    - Normal level II ultrasound, declined amniocentesis

© 2010 AWHONN 82

pruritic urticarial papules plaques of pregnancy.

Margaret (cont.):
Admission Tracing

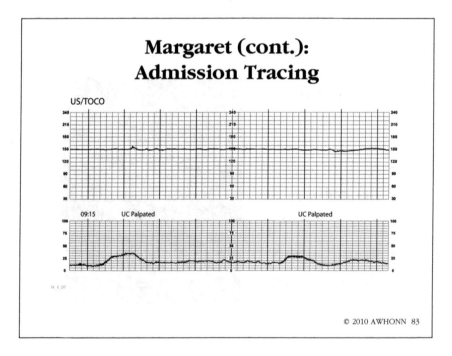

© 2010 AWHONN 83

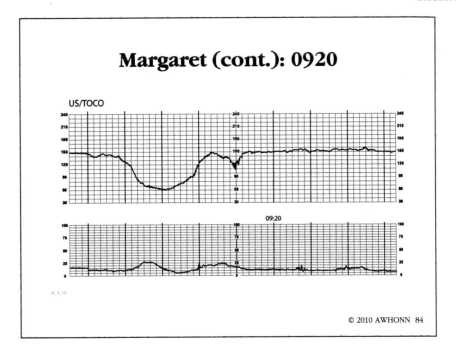

_____

_____

_____

_____

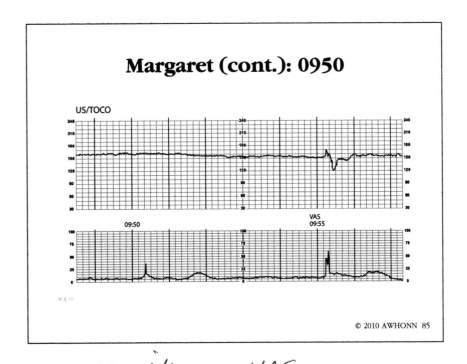

_____ variable c̄ VAS _____

_____

_____

_____

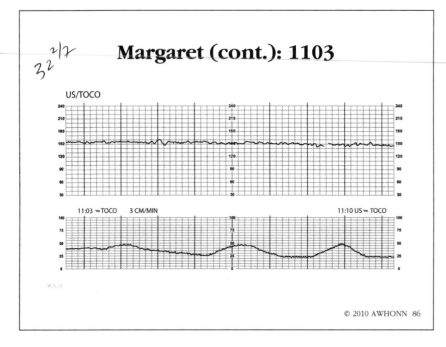

$3^2 \, {}^{2/7}$

Margaret (cont.): 1103

US/TOCO

11:03 ⇝ TOCO   3 CM/MIN   11:10 US ⇝ TOCO

W_8_12

© 2010 AWHONN 86

_____

_____

_____

_____

Margaret: Outcome

- Delivered at 1152

- Viable female infant:
  - Apgars 2/6/7
  - Cystic formations on umbilical cord
  - No signs of placental abruption

© 2010 AWHONN 87

_____

_____

_____

_____

Summary

- Antepartum fetal testing is a valuable and important component of prenatal care, particularly for at-risk women.

- The goal is to identify techniques that are user friendly, minimally invasive and yield the most useful information.

_____

_____

_____

_____

Fetal Cardiac Arrhythmias

© 2010 AWHONN 89

Why Study Fetal Arrhythmias?

 rare

- Fetal arrhythmias can:
  - Affect fetal cardiac output, FHR and pattern
  - Make tracing interpretation challenging

- Knowledge can facilitate assessment, as well as patient and family education

© 2010 AWHONN 90

Definition of Arrhythmia

- An arrhythmia is any irregularity of the fetal cardiac rhythm or any regular rhythm that remains outside the general range of 110–160 bpm.
- Two broad categories:
  - Variations in the R-R intervals: normal P-QRS pattern
  - Patterns that have disordered impulse formation, impulse conduction or both

© 2010 AWHONN 91

Cardiac and Conduction System Development

Weeks Gestation	Developmental Milestones
3	Tubular heart beating
4	Tube folds; atrial/ventricular septa and SA node forming
5	AV node and bundle of His forming; atria and ventricular septa
6	Valves forming; coronary circulation established
8–10	Septa fully formed; flow determines size

© 2010 AWHONN 92

Comparison of Cardiac Characteristics

Factor	Fetus	Adult
Contractile mass	30%	60%
Calcium transport	Altered	Fully functional
Cardiac pressures	High on right side (atrium)	High on left side
Cardiac output (CO)	RV output + LV output	LV output

© 2010 AWHONN 93

Properties of Cardiac Cells

- Automaticity:
  - Ability to spontaneously contract without neural stimulation

- Excitability:
  - Ability to respond to electrical stimulus

- Conductivity:
  - Ability to conduct electrical impulse through cardiac cells

© 2010 AWHONN 94

Cardiac Conduction Physiology

Polarization
(resting state)

Na⁺

K⁺

Depolarization
(contracting)

K⁺

Na⁺

Repolarization
(return to resting state)

Na⁺

K⁺

© 2010 AWHONN 95

Cardiac Conduction System

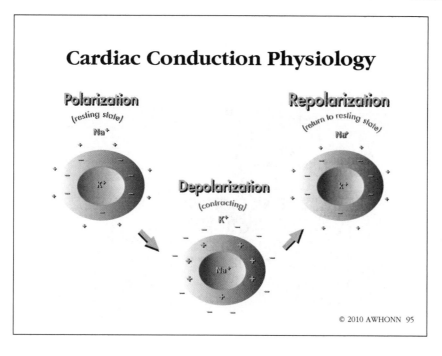

(110-160)

Sinoatrial (SA) node

Atrioventricular (AV) node

Right atrium

Right ventricle

Purkinje fibers

Normal EKG

Left atrium   40-60

Left ventricle

Right and left branches of AV bundle (bundle of His)   < 40

© 2010 AWHONN 96

Adult ECG pattern

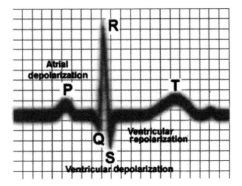

© 2010 AWHONN 97

Etiology of Arrhythmias

- Congenital heart defects:
  - SVT
  - Atrial flutter
  - Complete heart block
- Conduction system defects
- Disease processes such as:
  - Systemic lupus erythematosus(SLE)

© 2010 AWHONN 98

Sinus Node Variants: Tachycardia

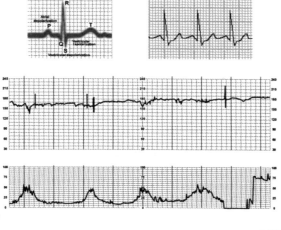

© 2010 AWHONN 99

maternal hyperthyroid
fetal anemia
hypoxia
maternal fever
pain / anxiety / stress

Sinus Node Variants: Bradycardia

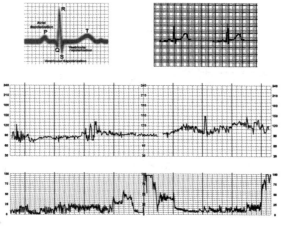

© 2010 AWHONN 100

Lupus - antibodies ans placenta + attack heart
block compression
fetal hypoxia
hypothyroidism

Mary, 34 Years Old, $G_1 P_0$, 41 Weeks' Gestation

- Family history: negative
- Medical/surgical history: negative
- Married and has support
- Pregnancy has been uncomplicated
- SROM, clear fluid, 12 hr. before admission
- Fetal movement present
- Mild, irregular uterine contractions

© 2010 AWHONN 101

Mary (cont.): Admission Tracing

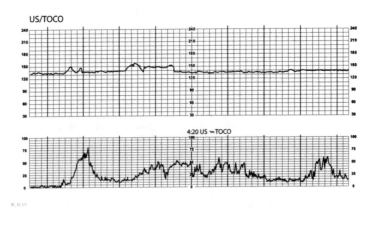

US/TOCO

4:20 US ∼TOCO

© 2010 AWHONN 102

Mary (cont.): 0445

US/TOCO

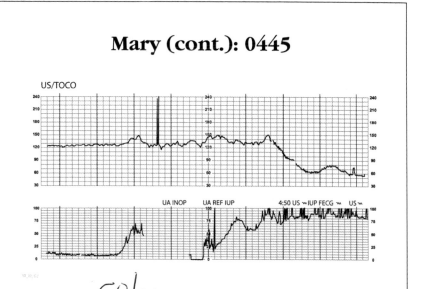

UA INOP   UA REF IUP   4:50 US ⌇IUP FECG ⌇   US ⌇

50/30

© 2010 AWHONN 103

, anaphylaxis

Mary (cont.): 0455

FSE/IUPC

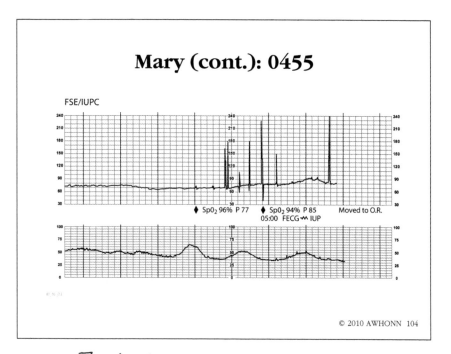

◆ SpO₂ 96% P 77   ◆ SpO₂ 94% P 85   Moved to O.R.
                    05:00 FECG ⌇ IUP

© 2010 AWHONN 104

Terbutaline x 2 doses
(vasodilator , can further
tank BP)

Mary (cont.): 0505

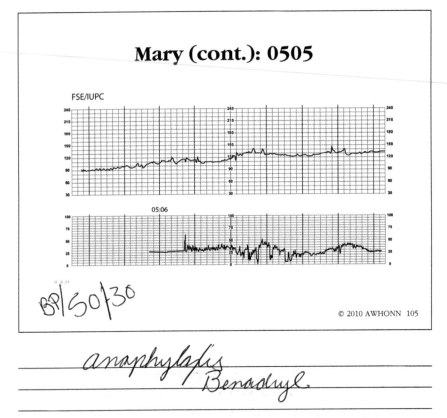

FSE/IUPC

05:06

© 2010 AWHONN 105

BP 50/30

anaphylafis
Benadryl

Mary (cont.): 0510

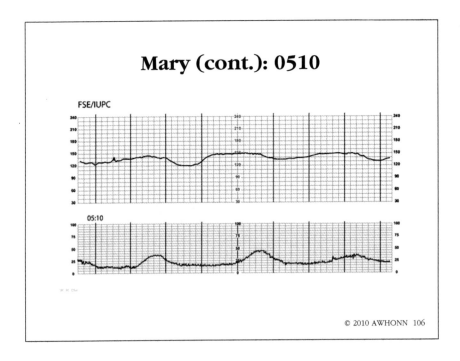

FSE/IUPC

05:10

© 2010 AWHONN 106

Mary (cont.): 0525

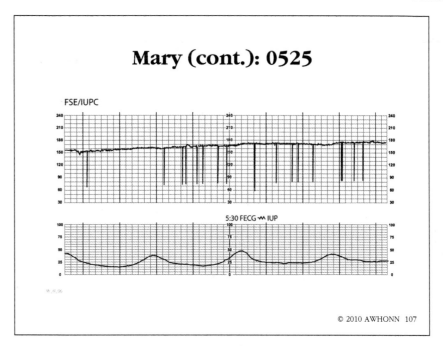

© 2010 AWHONN 107

auscultate c̄ petocone
US visualization
— artifact

Mary (cont.): 1035
Five Hours Since Last Tracing

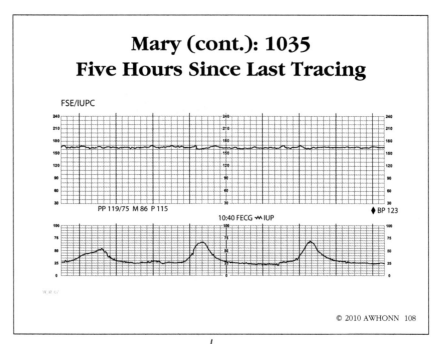

© 2010 AWHONN 108

C/S

↑ extra beats
baseline

↓ pauses

PAC /

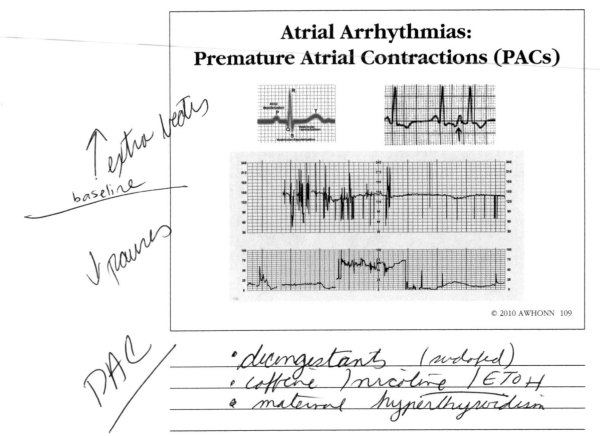

• decongestants (sudofed)
• caffeine / nicotine / ETOH
• maternal hyperthyroidism

240-260 bpm

high baseline
minimal variability

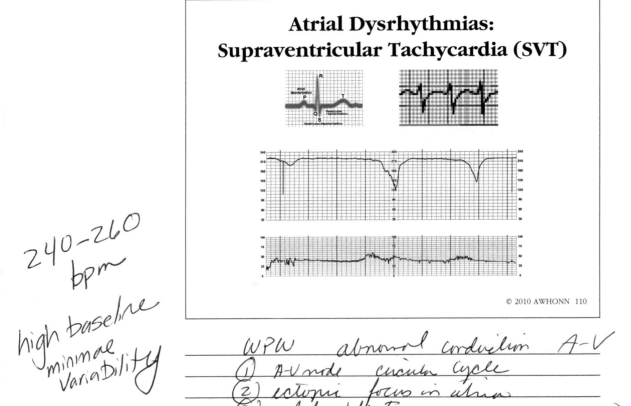

WPW abnormal conduction A-V
① A-V node circular cycle
② ectopic focus in atria
③ afib / flutter
④ beta symp drugs or cocaine

Esperanza, 25 Years Old, G_1 P_0, 24 Weeks' Gestation

- Family history: negative
- Medical/surgical history: negative
- Current pregnancy:
  - First prenatal visit
- Psychosocial history:
  - Unmarried
  - Migrant worker
  - Does not speak English

© 2010 AWHONN 111

Esperanza (cont.): Assessment Process

- Auscultated FHR >200 bpm × 2
- Referred to a tertiary center:
  - Fetal echocardiogram
  - Ultrasound
- Gestational age now 24 5/7 weeks

© 2010 AWHONN 112

Esperanza (cont.)

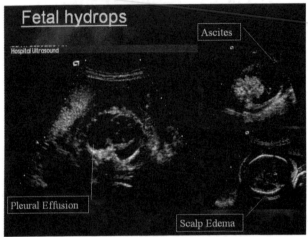

Used with permission OBGYN.net www.obgyn.net
Author Martin Necas

© 2010 AWHONN 113

Esperanza (cont.):
Treatment Plan

- Admitted to labor and delivery
- Digoxin therapy planned to convert rhythm
- Continuous maternal and fetal heart monitoring initiated
- Plan for continued care and evaluation of therapy explained

© 2010 AWHONN 114

Esperanza (cont.)

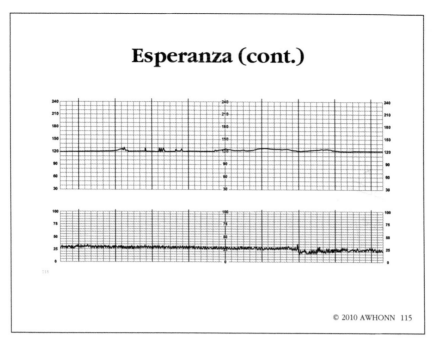

Esperanza (cont.)

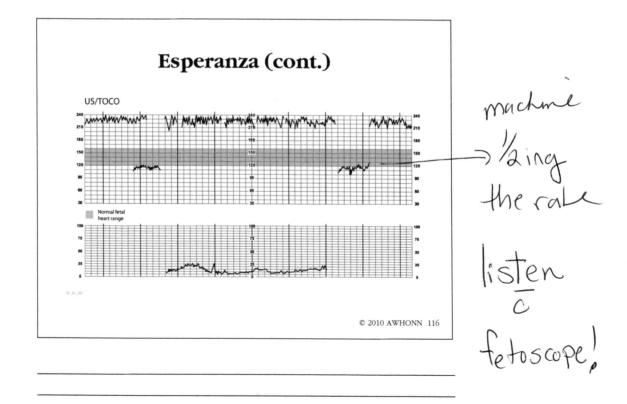

machine
→ ½ ing
the rate

listen
c̄
fetoscope!

Esperanza (cont.): Outcome

- Fetus converted to sinus rhythm within five days
- Digoxin continued on outpatient basis, then tapered off
- Delivered baby girl at 39 weeks:
  - 7 lb, 8 oz, (3,402 grams)
  - Apgars 9/9 at 1 and 5 minutes

© 2010 AWHONN 117

_____
_____
_____
_____

Atrial Arrhythmias: Atrial Flutter

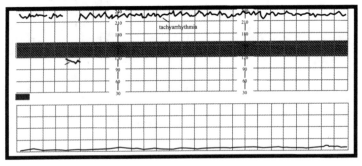

© 2010 AWHONN 118

300 bpm

reentry cycle
atrial wall ; atrial defects

Junctional and Ventricular Arrhythmias: AV Node Blocks

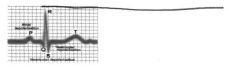

First Degree AV Block

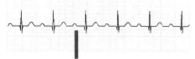

Second Degree AV Block

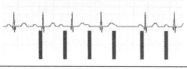

© 2010 AWHONN 119

below the atria

1st prolonged PR interval

2 type I longer, longer, drop

type II random drop

Junctional and Ventricular Arrhythmias: Third Degree AV Node Block

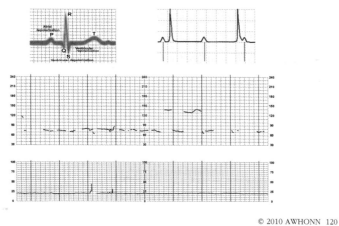

© 2010 AWHONN 120

impulse originate @ AV node

dissociation of SA + AV nodes

structure defects

Lupus, RA, CMV, APS

antiphospholipid syndrome

Junctional and Ventricular Arrhythmias: Premature Ventricular Contractions

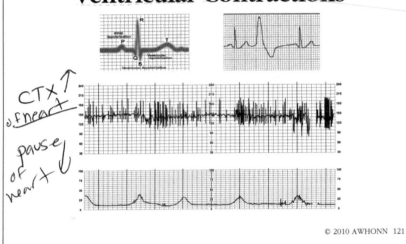

CTX ↑
of heart

pause
of
heart ↓

© 2010 AWHONN 121

myocarditis   hypokalemia
dig tox
cocaine/nicotine/ETOH
hydrops

Potential Consequences of Fetal Arrhythmias

Potential continuum of consequences:

- No apparent effect
- ✳ Fetal hydrops
- ✳ Death

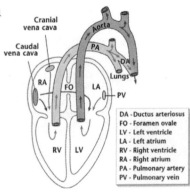

DA - Ductus arteriosus
FO - Foramen ovale
LV - Left ventricle
LA - Left atrium
RV - Right ventricle
RA - Right atrium
PA - Pulmonary artery
PV - Pulmonary vein

© 2010 AWHONN 122

Diagnosing Arrhythmias

- Spectral Doppler and color flow mapping
- Fetal echocardiography
- M-mode echocardiography
- Pulsed Doppler echocardiography

© 2010 AWHONN 123

Treatment of Arrhythmias

PACs, PVCs	Avoid caffeine/sympathomimetic medications/illicit drugs
Atrial flutter SVT	Administer digoxin Consider other antiarrhythmic medications
AV block	Consider sympathomimetic medications, betamethasone
Consider delivery for worsening fetal condition regardless of gestational age or deliver at term if stable	

© 2010 AWHONN 124

Arrhythmia: Conclusion

- Rare incidence
- Diagnostic and follow-up testing during prenatal period
- Assessment of impact of ↓ fetal cardiac output on fetal well-being
- Treatment plan based on specific rhythm
- Variable outcomes

© 2010 AWHONN 125

Dynamic Physiologic Response Model and Complex Case Scenarios

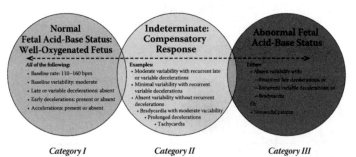

Normal Fetal Acid-Base Status: Well-Oxygenated Fetus	Indeterminate: Compensatory Response	Abnormal Fetal Acid-Base Status
All of the following: • Baseline rate: 110–160 bpm • Baseline variability: moderate • Late or variable decelerations: absent • Early decelerations: present or absent • Accelerations: present or absent	**Examples:** • Moderate variability with recurrent late or variable decelerations • Minimal variability with recurrent variable decelerations • Absent variability without recurrent decelerations • Bradycardia with moderate variability • Prolonged decelerations • Tachycardia	Either: • Absent variability with: —Recurrent late decelerations; or —Recurrent variable decelerations; or —Bradycardia Or: • Sinusoidal pattern
Category I	*Category II*	*Category III*

© 2010 AWHONN 126

Maya, 28 Years Old, $G_1 P_0$, 27 4/7 Weeks' Gestation, PPROM

- Family history: mother has hypertension
- Medical history: appendectomy age 15
- Previous pregnancies: denies
- Psychosocial history:
  - Dropped out of high school
  - Married, good support network
- Leaking clear amniotic fluid on admission

© 2010 AWHONN 127

Maya (cont.): NST Day Five

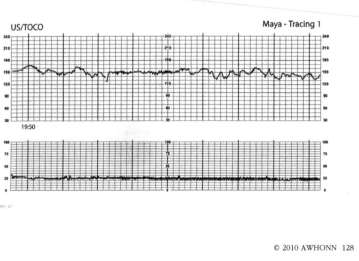

US/TOCO   Maya - Tracing 1

19:50

© 2010 AWHONN 128

Maya (cont.): 22 Hours Later, 1732

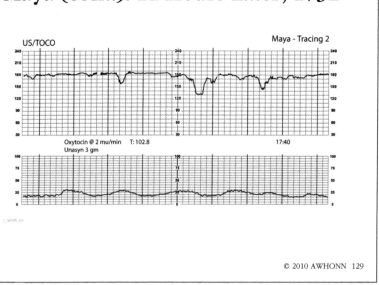

US/TOCO   Maya - Tracing 2

Oxytocin @ 2 mu/min   T: 102.8   17:40
Unasyn 3 gm

© 2010 AWHONN 129

Maya (cont.): 1750

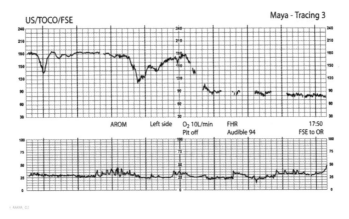

US/TOCO/FSE   Maya - Tracing 3

AROM   Left side   O₂ 10L/min   FHR   17:50
                          Pit off   Audible 94   FSE to OR

© 2010 AWHONN 130

FHM in the Preterm Fetus

- The physiologic responses are dependent on the stage of fetal development.

- The physiologic responses and tolerance to stress differ from those of the term fetus.

© 2010 AWHONN 131

Preterm FHR Characteristics

- The FHR baseline may be higher.
- Accelerations may be of lower amplitude.
- Variability may be decreased.
- Decelerations occur more frequently.

variables
28-30 wks.

© 2010 AWHONN 132

FHM in the Preterm Fetus

- Magnesium sulfate: decreases the FHR variability and acceleration amplitude
- Beta-sympathomimetics: tachycardia in both the mother and fetus
- Indomethacin, other prostaglandin inhibitors and calcium channel blockers: minimal effects

© 2010 AWHONN 133

Preterm Fetal Tolerance
to Stress

- Preterm fetus is more likely to be subjected to hypoxia.

- Preterm FHR patterns progress more rapidly to acidosis with disrupted oxygenation.

- Variable decelerations and tachycardia with loss of variability are associated with acidosis and low Apgar scores in the preterm fetus.

(Freeman et al., 2003)

© 2010 AWHONN 134

Sally, 20 Years Old,
$G_2 P_{0101}$, 35 Weeks Gestation

- Family history:
  - Mother—hypertension
  - Both parents—congestive heart failure (CHF)
  - Maternal grandmother—type 2 diabetes
- Medical history:
  - Chlamydia four years prior to pregnancy
  - Smokes ½ pack/day
  - Allergic to penicillin
  - Previous surgery—wisdom teeth extraction

© 2010 AWHONN 135

hx preeclampsia

Sally (cont.): Current Pregnancy

Gestation	Assessment	Vital Signs/Labs
35 weeks	C/o faintness, nausea, scotoma No edema 1+ reflexes	BP 136/96 Wt: 160 lb Negative urine protein
37 weeks	2–3+ reflexes 2+ pitting edema Facial edema	BP 138/84–153/114 range Wt: 161 lb Trace urine protein

© 2010 AWHONN 136

Sally (cont.): Three Days Later

Gestation	Assessment	Vital Signs/Labs
37 3/7 weeks	Headache, 1+ bilateral patellar reflexes	BP range 136/102–133/83 2+ urine protein

© 2010 AWHONN 137

Sally (cont.): Admission Data

- Admitted with bright red bleeding, leaking fluid and abdominal pain
- VS:
  - BP 183/105, P 130, R 24, T 98.9°F (37.1°C)
- Patellar reflexes: 3+; 0 clonus
- Unable to void

© 2010 AWHONN 138

Sally (cont.): Laboratory Values

- WBC: 15.23×10^9/L
- RBC: 3.54×10^{12}/L
- Hct: 29.7%
- Hgb: 9.0 g/dL
- Platelets: 98K/mm³
- PT: 9.9 secs
- PTT: 30 secs

- Fibrinogen: 300 mg/dL
- Uric acid: 7.1 mg/dL
- Alk phos: 253 IU/mL
- AST: 45 IU
- ALT: 28 IU
- LDH: 542 IU
- Urine protein: 3+
- Urine drug screen neg

© 2010 AWHONN 139

Sally (cont.): Admission Tracing

US/TOCO

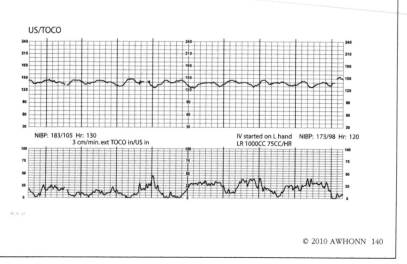

NIBP: 183/105 Hr: 130   IV started on L hand   NIBP: 173/98 Hr: 120
      3 cm/min. ext TOCO in/US in   LR 1000CC 75CC/HR

© 2010 AWHONN 140

Sally (cont.): 0011

US/TOCO

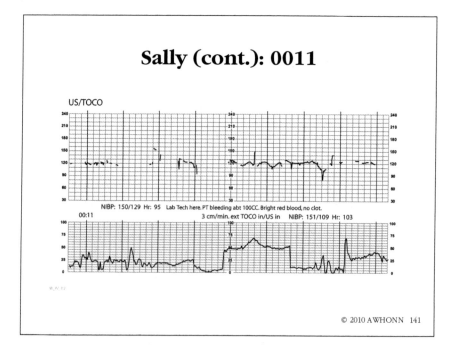

NIBP: 150/129 Hr: 95   Lab Tech here. PT bleeding abt 100CC. Bright red blood, no clot.
00:11   3 cm/min. ext TOCO in/US in   NIBP: 151/109 Hr: 103

© 2010 AWHONN 141

Sally (cont.): 0020

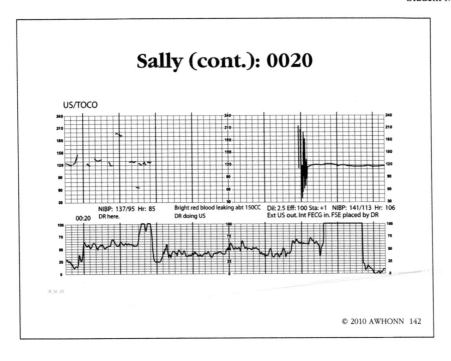

US/TOCO

NIBP: 137/95 Hr: 85   Bright red blood leaking abt 150CC   Dil: 2.5 Eff: 100 Sta: +1   NIBP: 141/113 Hr: 106
00:20   DR here.   DR doing US   Ext US out. Int FECG in. FSE placed by DR

© 2010 AWHONN 142

Sally (cont.): 0029

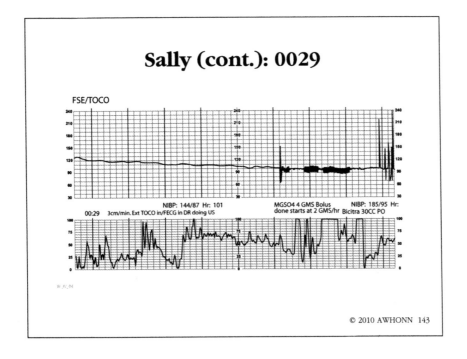

FSE/TOCO

NIBP: 144/87 Hr: 101   MGSO4 4 GMS Bolus   NIBP: 185/95 Hr:
00:29   3cm/min. Ext TOCO in/FECG in DR doing US   done starts at 2 GMS/hr   Bicitra 30CC PO

© 2010 AWHONN 143

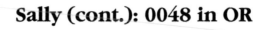

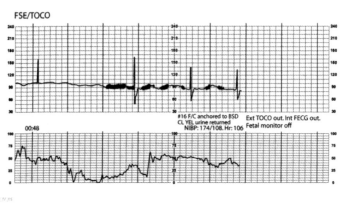

Sally (cont.): 0048 in OR

FSE/TOCO

#16 F/C anchored to BSD
CL YEL urine returned
NIBP: 174/108. Hr: 106

Ext TOCO out. Int FECG out.
Fetal monitor off

00:48

© 2010 AWHONN 144

Sally (cont.): Outcome

- Primary cesarean section with general anesthesia at 0103
- Female infant; 4 lb, 11 oz (2,126 g)
- Apgars 0/0/1/3
- Full resuscitation x 11 minutes
- Baby to NICU
- Had one mild seizure in NICU

© 2010 AWHONN 145

Sally (cont.): Outcome

Umbilical arterial blood gas results:
- pH   6.55
- pCO_2 127.8 mmHg
- pO_2 11.4 mmHg
- HCO_3 10.6 mmHg
- BD   32 mmol/L

© 2010 AWHONN 146

Sally (cont.): Outcome
Couvelaire Uterus

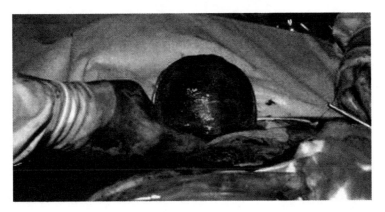

© 2010 AWHONN 147

Abruptio Placentae

- Pathophysiology:
  - Premature separation of placenta
- Risk factors:
  - Hypertension
  - Cigarette smoking
  - Substance abuse
  - Trauma
  - Rapid decompression of the uterus

© 2010 AWHONN 148

Sally (cont.): Outcome

- Sally discharged home on day four

- Infant discharged home on day 19:
  - No apparent deficits on discharge
  - At one year of age, no neurological deficits noted

© 2010 AWHONN 149

Dhamra, 41 Years Old, $G_4 P_{0210}$, 23 2/7 Weeks' Gestation

- Medical history:
  - Frequent urinary tract infections
- Obstetrical history:
  - Two preterm deliveries at 22 and 23 weeks
- Current pregnancy:
  - Twin gestation (diamniotic/dichorionic)
  - Bleeding in the first trimester
  - Shortened cervix on ultrasound

© 2010 AWHONN 150

Dhamra (cont.)

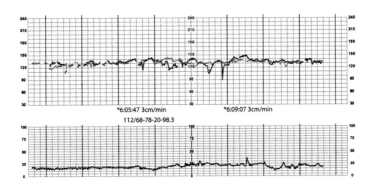

*6:05:47 3cm/min   *6:09:07 3cm/min
112/68-78-20-98.3

© 2010 AWHONN 151

Dhamra (cont.)

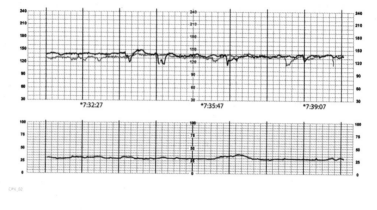

Surgery in Pregnancy

- No data for specific recommendations for fetal monitoring

- FHM should be individualized

- FHM may be technically difficult to perform

FHR Heart Rate Interpretation During Surgery

- Changes in baseline variability or the new onset of decelerations may be an early warning sign
- Documentation specific to procedure
- Qualified staff member for interpretation
- Unit policy and procedure

© 2010 AWHONN 154

Nadine, 15 Years Old
G_1P_0, 36 2/7 Weeks' Gestation

- Family history:
  - Unremarkable

- Medical history:
  - History of asthma last two years
  - Heart murmur
  - Chronic hematuria

© 2010 AWHONN 155

Nadine: Current Pregnancy

Current pregnancy:

- C/o dizziness for past two days
- C/o "wet panties" since 0530
- Labs: all within normal limits
- ABO/Rh - A negative
- Hgb: 13.3 g/dL
- HbsAG, HIV, Chlamydia, GC all neg
- + Group B Strep at 32 weeks by urine culture

© 2010 AWHONN 156

Nadine (cont.): Admission Data

- Fetal movement normal
- No uterine activity; no bleeding
- VS: BP 145/81, P 78, R 18, T 99.2°F (37.2°C)
- SVE: 2 cm/50%/-2
- Penicillin G 5 million units by IV piggyback
- Oxytocin started at 3 milliunits/minute

© 2010 AWHONN 157

Nadine (cont.): Admission Tracing

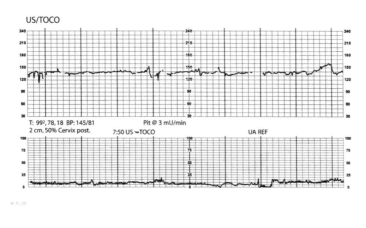

Nadine (cont.): 1316

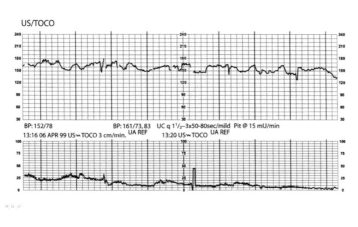

Nadine (cont.): 1900

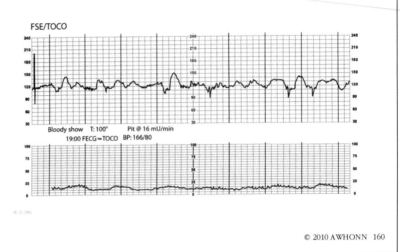

FSE/TOCO

Bloody show   T: 100°   Pit @ 16 mU/min
19:00 FECG~TOCO   BP: 166/80

Nadine (cont.): 1910

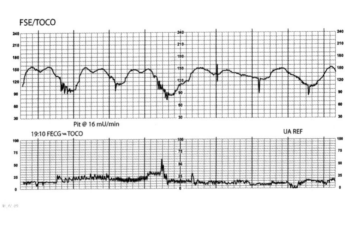

FSE/TOCO

Pit @ 16 mU/min
19:10 FECG~TOCO   UA REF

Nadine (cont.): 2000

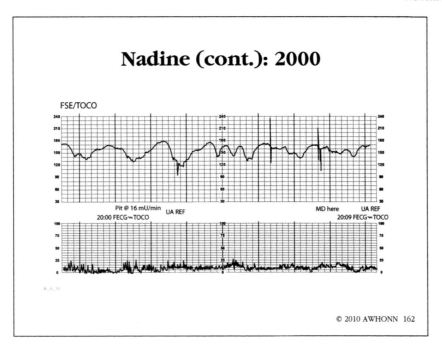

Nadine (cont.): 2013

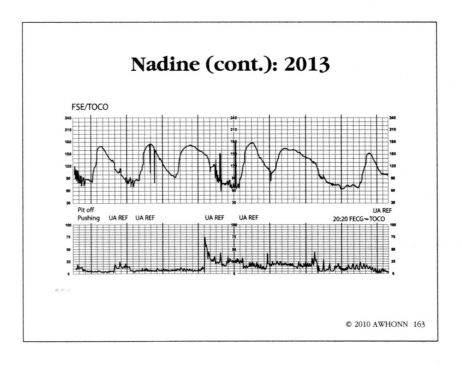

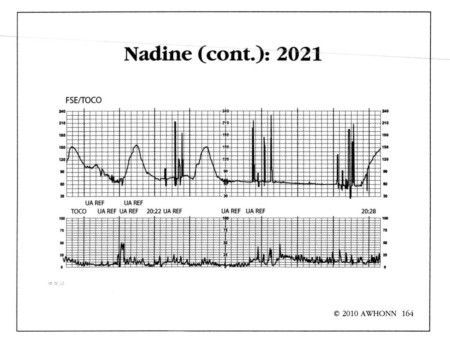

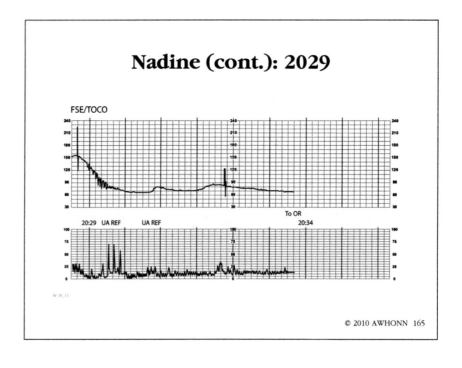

Nadine (cont.): Outcome

- Cesarean birth at 8:41 p.m.
- Female infant, 7 lb, 4 oz (3,288.5 g)
- Apgars 1/1/intubated
- Enlarging cephalohematoma noted
- Full code × 20 minutes; pronounced in OR
- Uterine rupture of 50%

© 2010 AWHONN 166

Clinical Signs of Uterine Rupture

- Presence of late or variable decelerations followed by bradycardia in the fetus
- Loss of fetal station
- Constant abdominal pain
- Change in uterine shape
- Cessation of contractions
- Hematuria

© 2010 AWHONN 167

Ginny, 30 Years Old
$G_3 P_{1011}$, 37 5/7 Weeks' Gestation

- Family history:
  - Mother type 2 diabetes
  - Father bladder cancer

- Medical history
  - History of human papilloma virus (HPV)
  - Latex allergy

© 2010 AWHONN 168

Ginny (cont.): History

- Previous pregnancies:
  - Miscarriage at eight weeks
  - Preeclampsia, postpartum hemorrhage
- Current pregnancy:
  - Sudden onset of gross hematuria, nausea
  - Hospitalized for renal evaluation
  - Hydronephrotic kidney identified
  - Stent placed

© 2010 AWHONN 169

Ginny (cont.): Admission Data

Laboratory tests:
- WBC: $10.0 \times 10^9/L$
- Hct: 36%
- Platelets: 312K mm^3

Ginny (cont.): Admission Data

- Vital signs:
  - BP 129/80, P 100, R 18, T 99°F (37.2°C)
- Cervix closed, thick; high station; cephalic
- Contractions:
  - Q 3–4 minutes; duration 60 seconds; moderate, soft resting tone
- FHR baseline: 150 bpm, minimal variability

Ginny (cont.): Admission Tracing

US/TOCO

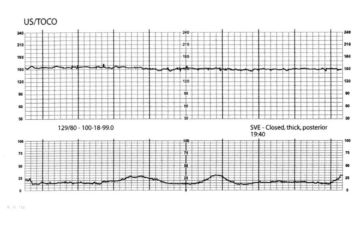

129/80 - 100-18-99.0

SVE - Closed, thick, posterior
19:40

© 2010 AWHONN 172

Ginny (cont.): 0028

US/TOCO

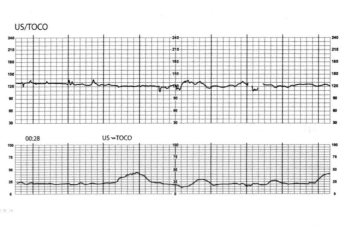

00:28   US ∿TOCO

© 2010 AWHONN 173

Ginny (cont.): 0238

32
108/60 , 82

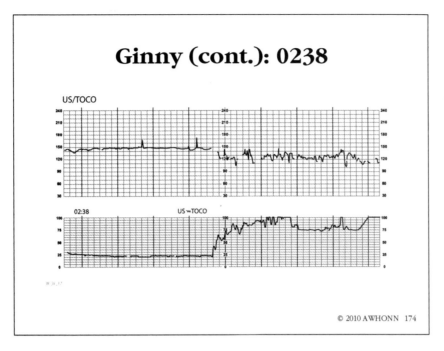

US/TOCO

02:38   US ~TOCO

_____

_____

_____

_____

Ginny (cont.): 0418 and 0805

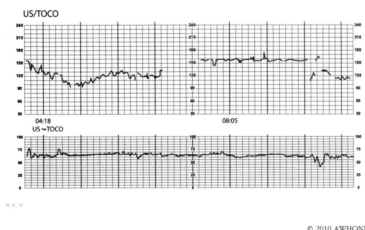

US/TOCO

04:18   08:05

US ~TOCO

_____

_____

_____

_____

Ginny (cont.): 0812

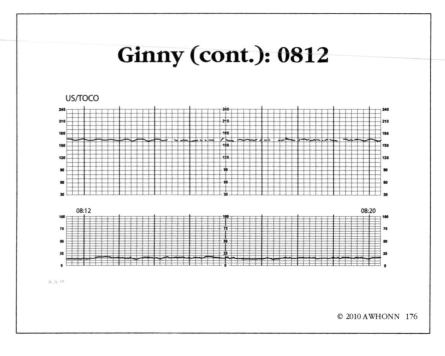

Ginny (cont.): 1119

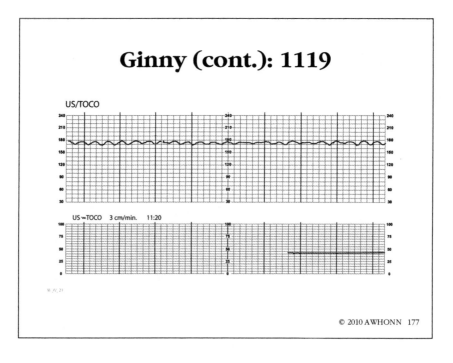

Ginny (cont.): 1409

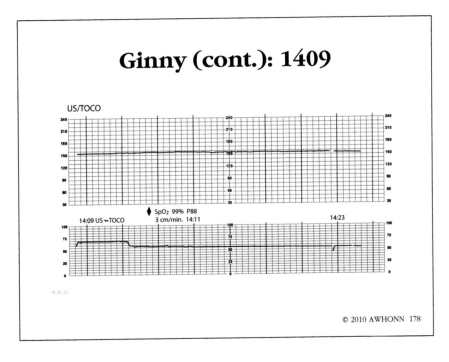

Ginny (cont.): 1500

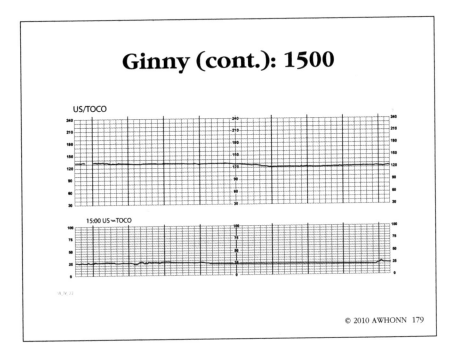

Ginny (cont.): 1540

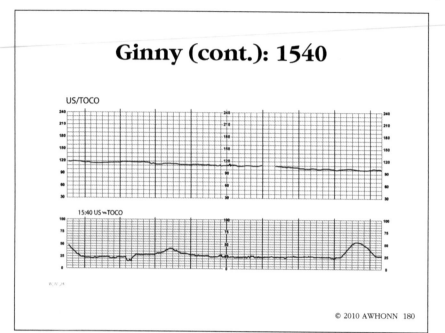

US/TOCO

15:40 US TOCO

Ginny (cont.): Outcome

- Cesarean birth at 1559, general anesthesia
- Male infant, 7 lb, 14 oz (3,571 g)
- Neonatal laboratory values:
  - Hematocrit: 19%
  - Hemoglobin: 6.3 gm/dL
  - Red blood cells: 1.77×10^{12}/L
  - Platelets: 149,000K
- Apgars 1/1/1/2/4/5/7

Ginny (cont.): Outcome

Umbilical arterial cord gases:

- pH   6.77
- pCO_2 58.0
- pO_2 19.0
- HCO_3 9.0
- BD   32

© 2010 AWHONN 182

Sinusoidal Patterns

- Medication-induced pattern:
  - Short duration
  - Preceded and followed by normal characteristics
- Condition-specific pattern:
  - No accelerations
  - No response to uterine contractions, fetal movement or stimulation

© 2010 AWHONN 183

Summary

Normal Fetal Acid-Base Status: Well-Oxygenated Fetus

All of the following:
- Baseline rate: 110–160 bpm
- Baseline variability: moderate
- Late or variable decelerations: absent
- Early decelerations: present or absent
- Accelerations: present or absent

Category I

Indeterminate: Compensatory Response

Examples:
- Moderate variability with recurrent late or variable decelerations
- Minimal variability with recurrent variable decelerations
- Absent variability without recurrent decelerations
- Bradycardia with moderate variability
- Prolonged decelerations
- Tachycardia

Category II

Abnormal Fetal Acid-Base Status

Either:
- Absent variability with:
  —Recurrent late decelerations, or
  —Recurrent variable decelerations, or
  —Bradycardia
Or
- Sinusoidal pattern

Category III

© 2010 AWHONN 184

Communication, Documentation and Risk Management

© 2010 AWHONN 185

What Do You See?

© 2010 AWHONN 186

Patient Safety Initiatives

- Quality patient care that optimizes patient outcomes
- Communication among healthcare providers
- Standardized terminology for fetal monitoring was recommended by JCAHO in the July 2004 Sentinel Event Alert #30
- Use of consistent FHM terminology among professional associations

© 2010 AWHONN 187

Root Causes of Perinatal Deaths and Injuries—JCAHO 1995–2004

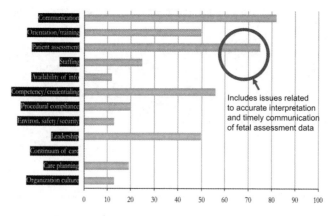

(Joint Commission on Accreditation of Healthcare Organizations [JCAHO], 2004)

© 2010 AWHONN 188

Effective Communication

- Speaking clearly
- Being courteous and professional
- Presenting facts in a methodical or chronological format
- Asking for clarification if communication or orders are not clear
- Communicating recommendations for care

© 2010 AWHONN 189

SBAR

- Situation: What is going on with the patient?
- Background: What is the key clinical background or context?
- Assessment: What do I think the problem is?
- Recommendation: What do I recommend or what do I want to do?

© 2010 AWHONN 190

Safe Patient Handoffs

- Face-to-face communication
- Assess patient status together
- Limit interruptions during handoffs
- Solicit outgoing team's opinions about patient status and potential for changes in condition
- Ensure that key tasks are not left for oncoming team
- Use role-playing to teach new staff

© 2010 AWHONN 191

Strategies for Successful Communication

- Basic tenet of clinical practice
- Use applicable evidence or published standards and guidelines
- Examples of sources of standards and guidelines:
  - AWHONN
  - ACOG
  - ACNM
  - AAP

© 2010 AWHONN 192

Communication and Areas of Risk

- Failure to properly assess maternal-fetal status
- Failure to recognize a worsening condition
- Failure to provide appropriate interventions with a Category II/III tracing
- Failure to communicate maternal–fetal status

© 2010 AWHONN 193

Communication and Areas of Risk

- Failure to communicate maternal–fetal status
- Failure of MD/CNM to respond appropriately when notified of a Category II/III tracing
- Failure to use chain of command or authority to resolve issues effectively

© 2010 AWHONN 194

Strategies to Reduce FHM Liability

- Development of clear guidelines for fetal monitoring of potentially high-risk patients, including clinical protocols for interpretation of fetal heart rate tracings
- Education of nurses, residents, nurse midwives and physicians to use standardized terminology in communicating abnormal fetal heart rate tracings
- Review of organizational policies regarding availability of key personnel for emergency interventions

© 2010 AWHONN 195

Communication and Informed Consent

- Form of communication
- Documentation:
  - Patient's signature
  - Witness's signature
  - Date and time
  - Documentation of the conversation with the patient

© 2010 AWHONN 196

Main Elements
of Informed Consent

- Discussion of indications for tests or treatment
- Description of nature and purpose of tests or treatment
- Description of principal benefits and risks
- Discussion of diagnostic or treatment alternatives
- Description of common consequences of forgoing recommended tests or treatment

© 2010 AWHONN 197

Completing the Consent Process

- Allow time for patient to understand the information
- Encourage patient to ask questions
- Provide answers the patient can comprehend at his or her educational level
- Validate the patient's understanding of the procedure

Adapted from Woods & Rozovsky, 2003

© 2010 AWHONN 198

Documentation of FHR Characteristics

Auscultation	Electronic Monitoring
Rate	Rate
Rhythm	Variability
Increases & decreases	Periodic & episodic changes
	Pattern evolution
Associated clinical findings	
Communications	

© 2010 AWHONN 199

Documenting Uterine Activity

Palpation	Tocodynamometer	Intrauterine Pressure Catheter
Frequency In minutes from beginning of one contraction to the beginning of the next		
Duration In seconds: average length of contractions		
Soft or firm	**Resting Tone** By palpation: soft, firm	mmHg *and* palpation
Mild, moderate, strong	**Intensity** Mild, moderate, strong	mmHg *and* palpation
Descriptive Degree of associated pain and maternal coping *Normal uterine activity* or *tachysystole*		

© 2010 AWHONN 200

Documentation of Interventions

- Maximize uterine blood flow
- Maximize umbilical circulation
- Maximize oxygenation
- Maintain appropriate uterine activity
- Support maternal coping and labor progress

© 2010 AWHONN 201

Documentation Frequency

- Determined by institutional guidelines
- Assessment
- Evaluation
- Documentation

© 2010 AWHONN 202

Frequency of EFM Assessments

AWHONN, 2009 AAP & ACOG, 2007*	Active First Stage	Active Second Stage
Normal labor	Every 30 minutes	Every 15 minutes
Risk factors present - Medical/OB risk - Oxytocin	Every 15 minutes	Every 5 minutes
SOGC, 2007*	Active First Stage	Active Second Stage
All women receiving EFM	Every 15 minutes	Every 5 minutes

* See the full text of the cited guidelines for exceptions, qualifications and further information

© 2010 AWHONN 203

Recommended Auscultation Frequency

	Latent Phase	Active First Stage	Active Second Stage
ACNM, 2007		Every 15–30 minutes	Every 5 minutes
AWHONN, 2008		Every 15–30 minutes	Every 5–15 minutes
ACOG & AAP, 2007		Every 15–30 minutes	Every 5 minutes
SOGC, 2007	At time of assessment and approximately every hour	Every 15–30 minutes	Every 15 Minutes then every 5 minutes once pushing begins

© 2010 AWHONN 204

Suggested FHR Assessments with Procedures and Events

- Rupture of membranes
- Ambulation of patient
  - Return from ambulation
  - To bathroom
- Administration of analgesia or anesthesia
- Level of maternal discomfort

- Cervical exams
- Character of bloody show
- Recognition of abnormal FHR patterns or uterine activity
- Medication administration

© 2010 AWHONN 205

Late Entries in the Medical Record

- **Why?**

- **When?**

- **How?**

© 2010 AWHONN 206

Documentation of Emergent Events

- Time FHR or maternal status changes

- Actions initiated for maternal or fetal resuscitation

- Continued assessment of responses to interventions

- Communication with team members and responses

- Chronologies of interventions performed (including by which personnel) for both mother and newborn

© 2010 AWHONN 207

Minimizing Liability Risk

Continuing education:
- Joint responsibility among nurses and employers
- Needed to:
  - Maintain competency in areas of practice
  - Obtain new knowledge
  - Incorporate new technology and skills into practice
  - Maintain awareness of current research as it applies to practice

© 2010 AWHONN 208

Additional Suggestions for Minimizing Liability Risk

- Use medical record audit tools
- Practice according to guidelines
- Participate in and promote multidisciplinary quality management and policy development

Simpson & Knox, 2003

© 2010 AWHONN 209

_____

_____

_____

_____

Rashona, 31 Years Old, $G_1 P_{000}$, 39 Weeks' Gestation

- Family history:
  - Unremarkable
- Medical/surgical history:
  - Latex allergy
- Psychosocial history:
  - Unremarkable
- Prenatal history:
  - Labs within normal range

© 2010 AWHONN 210

_____

_____

_____

_____

3/80/-1

Rashona (cont.): Admission Tracing 0620

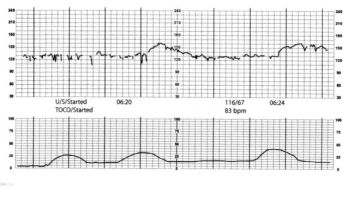

U/S/Started   06:20   116/67   06:24
TOCO/Started   83 bpm

_____

_____

_____

_____

Rashona (cont.): 1115

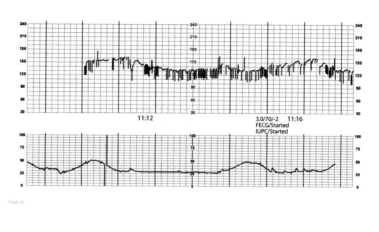

11:12   3.0/70/-2   11:16
                FECG/Started
                IUPC/Started

_____

_____

_____

_____

Rashona (cont.): 1545

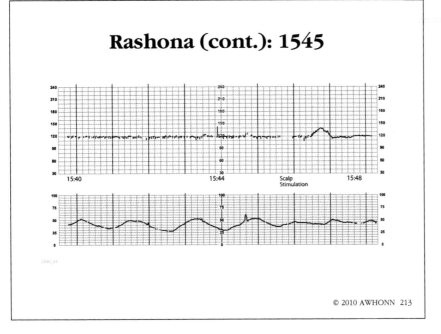

Scalp Stimulation

© 2010 AWHONN 213

4/80/-1
Tachysystole

Team Leader/Charge Nurse

- Leadership is important for optimizing positive outcomes
- Leadership skills:
  - Knowledge of principles
  - Clinical competence
  - Interpersonal skills

© 2010 AWHONN 214

Charge Nurse Role

- Clinical expert
- Skilled in delegation, supervision
- Consultant
- Advisor
- Arbitrator
- Triage expert
- Administrator

© 2010 AWHONN 215

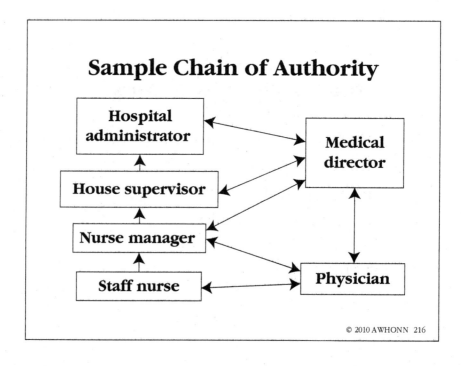

Sample Chain of Authority

© 2010 AWHONN 216

Rashona (cont.)

- Conversation outside room

- Charge nurse involved

- Review of unit oxytocin policy

© 2010 AWHONN 217

Rashona (cont.): 2150

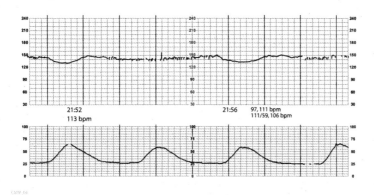

© 2010 AWHONN 218

Rashona (cont.): 2230

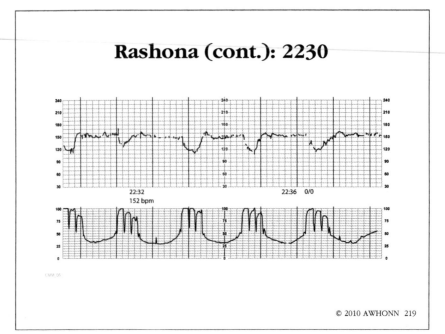

22:32
152 bpm
22:36 0/0

© 2010 AWHONN 219

Rashona (cont.): Outcome

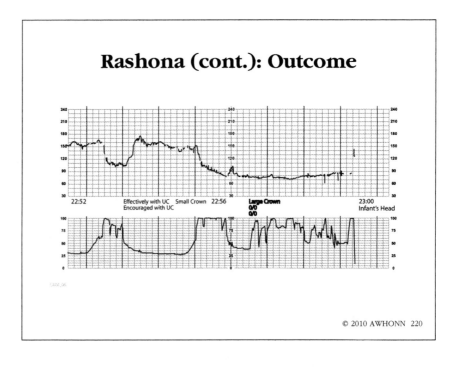

22:52 Effectively with UC Small Crown 22:56 Large Crown 23:00
Encouraged with UC   0/0   Infant's Head
                                             0/0

© 2010 AWHONN 220

Rashona (cont.): Outcome

- Spontaneous vaginal delivery
- Male 7 lb, 0 oz (3,175 g)
- Apgars 5 and 8
- Cord gases "clotted"
- Postpartum hemorrhage requiring misoprostol

© 2010 AWHONN 221

Clinical Decision Making

- Maternal-fetal physiology
- Physical assessment
- Patient interview
- Technology capabilities
- Core knowledge
- Communication
- Documentation

© 2010 AWHONN 222

_____

_____

_____

_____